BOOK IV

DECODING DEATH

METAPHYSICAL INTERPRETATION

O.M. KELLY

COPYRIGHT

Copyright © 2023 Margret Ann Kelly/O.M. Kelly
Series: Book IV (Revised)
First Published as Book IV in "Decoding the Mind of God",
Margret Ann Kelly/O.M. Kelly, Copyright © 2011.
ISBN: 978-0-6458487-0-0

All rights reserved. This book may not be reproduced, wholly or in part, or transmitted in any form whatsoever without written permission from the author, O.M. Kelly, www.elanea.com.

The author of this book does not dispense medical advice or prescribe the use of any technique as a form of treatment for physical, emotional, or medical problems without the advice of a physician, either directly or indirectly. The intent of the author is only to offer information of a general nature to help you in your quest for emotional and spiritual well-being. In the event you use any of the information in this book for yourself, which is your constitutional right, the author assumes no responsibility for your actions.

AUTHOR

Author O. M. Kelly, known as Omni to her clients and students is an accomplished author and international lecturer, on Metaphysics, Philosophy and understanding the Collective Consciousness. Omni consults for Member States of the European Commission as a Conciliation Advisor and Rhetoric Counsellor for other International Companies throughout Europe. Omni now resides on Australia's beautiful Gold Coast, writing books, and works as a Life Mentor and Business Coach.

Omni has dedicated her life to decoding the mysteries of the universe. With a deep knowledge of the biblical agenda, mythologies including ancient Egyptology, Asian principles, and metaphysical insights, Omni has discovered the secret that all stories share a coded hidden metaphysical language. Her seminal work, "Decoding the Mind of God", is a compilation of nine volumes of metaphysical information based on the research into the coded information of the Laws of the Universe, also known as the Collective Consciousness, and represents a groundbreaking contribution to our understanding of the metaphysical universe. Now, all nine volumes are being released as separate, revised books, each offering a unique perspective on the universe's workings. Omni's work has been widely acclaimed for its depth of insight, and her contributions to the field of metaphysics have been groundbreaking.

THIS BOOK

"Decoding Death" takes us on a transformative Metaphysical journey through the mysteries of the Universe. O.M. Kelly—known as Omni—provides an expanded horizon of possibilities, awareness, and an evolutionary perspective on dying and death.

In this book, Omni delves into a wide range of topics related to dying and death, from the loss of a loved one to a viewing of the afterlife. Omni has a unique ability to view the Laws of the Universe using her extraordinary state of heightened awareness and multi-dimensional perception and through the lens of metaphysics offers a unique perspective on the nature of death and what it means for the human experience.

Omni shares personal experiences and stories, including the passing of her late husband, brother, and parents, and offers a metaphysical insight for those dealing with loss and grief. She explores the transformational process of death and the potential for spiritual growth and enlightenment. The book explains that the human experience of death is part of a larger Universal process that is ultimately guided by a higher intelligence referred to as God (Laws of the Universe/ Collective Consciousness) or whatever name you prefer. Omni's exploration of death is both metaphysically comprehensive and thought-provoking, offering readers a deep and nuanced understanding of one of life's greatest mysteries. With chapters on the Three Doorways—Three Stages of Death, The Quantum Hologram—Why a partner dies for the other partner to progress in the "Journey of Life", The Passing to the Afterlife, and many other enlightening chapters, "Decoding Death" offers a unique viewpoint. By drawing on a range of religious, philosophical, and metaphysical perspectives, Omni offers a compelling vision of the human experience of death and its role in the larger Universal Law.

CONTENT

Introduction

Chapter One
The Loss Of A Loved One — Page 1

Chapter Two
Death Is Not An End—A Transition To A
Different State Of Consciousness — Page 3

Chapter Three
My Late Husband — Page 8

Chapter Four
The Passing Of Family, Spouses And Others
To Release The Soul's Energy — Page 11

Chapter Five
The Quantum Hologram—Why A Partner Dies
For The Other Partner To Progress In The
Journey Of Life — Page 19

Chapter Six
The Three Doorways—Three Stages Of Death — Page 24

Chapter Seven
The Passing To The Afterlife — Page 29

Chapter Eight
The Transformational Process — Page 31

Chapter Nine
Death: Accidents, Young Children, Your Thoughts — Page 33

Chapter Ten
When An Elderly Life Partner Dies — Page 38

Chapter Eleven
Interacting With The Soul — Page 41

Chapter Twelve
Death Is Of Your Design — Page 43

Chapter Thirteen
Suicide — Page 45

Chapter Fourteen
Near-Death Experiences, Visions, And
Out-Of-Body Experiences — Page 47

Chapter Fifteen
A Metaphysical Interpretation Of The Egyptian
Afterlife And The Interpretation Of The Three
Gods "EL", "AN", and "EA" Through Mythology — Page 52

Chapter Sixteen
Past Lives and Reincarnation—A Message From
Your Soul — Page 56

Chapter Seventeen
A Principal Law Of Shamanism — Page 61

Chapter Eighteen
Allow The Old Thoughts To Die To Your Past,
The Moment Of Death And Grieving — Page 64

Chapter Nineteen
Questions Regarding Energies And Entities — Page 67

Chapter Twenty
I Am My Temple — Page 72

Chapter Twenty One
The Afterlife For Adults — Page 75

Appendix A
Short Summary Question And Answer Format — Page 79

Appendix B
Remote Viewing And Astral Travelling — Page 92

Appendix C
Review Of Our Individual Universal Law And The
Laws Of The Universe — Page 94

Appendix D Brief Metaphysical Overview Of The
Brain/Mind/Levels of Consciousness — Page 104

Appendix E
Releasing The Past And Fears — Page 107

Other Books By O.M. Kelly (Omni) — Page 114

INTRODUCTION

Over the years, many people have asked me, through their innocence, to explain this sentience—or sentence—that we call "death". This book delves into the profound emotions of love and pain that shape our lives. The loss of a beloved partner after a lifetime of devotion can leave us feeling shattered and uncertain about our belief in self. As we confront the reality of our shared world coming to an end, we must learn to rely on our inner strength and face the unknown with courage. However, the codes of the Laws of the Universe offer us a new chapter in our personal growth, where we can rediscover our resilience. Love is a powerful force that transcends physical boundaries and persists beyond our lifetime. When we express love towards others, we emit a vibrational energy that can affect those around us and even influence the world. If we all embraced the power of love and allowed it to flow freely into our consciousness, we could transform the fabric of time and create a better world for all.

I have explained in this book, through the metaphysical codes, the understanding of death when members of our family die—our parents, siblings, spouses, children, and other relatives, and our friends, too. And, more importantly, through the codes, we understand the reason why the Laws of the Universe have added up to choose which one of us has earned the right to go on. We can begin to understand and see that God or whatever name you would prefer has a purpose by which every human must abide by. The Universe is never-ending. Just as we begin, so do we end: at the beginning. When we come through the wisdom of consciousness, we are a wonderment to our family, and then to ourselves, as we yearn to learn and to earn our emotional intelligence. We grow and have the opportunity to experience every facet of life while we are here. This eternal energy is everlasting, and it is freely available for you to have at your disposal the moment you ask yourself a question. That is the cycle of life. Death is just a new beginning. It is a repeat performance of what you have lived here; the only difference is that there is no ego to argue with you. Love is abounding and unconditional. Understand, accept, and have the ability now to act out in freedom and joy for the rest of your life.   Omni

CHAPTER ONE

The Loss Of A Loved One

Losing a loved one after what feels a million lifetimes of service to each other can shatter one's belief in self. We are the ones who are left behind, and now we have to change our old reliance and face the fact that our world that we shared with one another has finished. The Laws of the Universe have initiated us into the next paragraph of our hidden library, and our next venture will be to regain our strength and move on. Love never dies; it continues to live on throughout our lifetime, and it is always regenerated into a new life form of compatible energy.

As we love, we automatically deliver the same vibrations to the person standing beside us, and that powerful energy changes their feelings. They are then carried through the wind, or the Breath of God, to vibrate around those who are searching for love. If every person allowed their love to flow freely out into the consciousness, we would change the molecular structure of time, which would ease the pressure of millions of people who are living their life, but who have yet to understand the design that love creates for the whole planet.

Why are our children taken from us before they have reached maturity? We feel that our children have been robbed of their own experience. Many parents have told me that their child had to forfeit their life and want to know the reason why. What are the Laws of the Universe up to? What is God up to? We understand and accept death so much more easily when an elderly person dies, as we are aware that they have lived their lives mostly to their satisfaction.

I have been entrusted with the responsibility of sharing with you the Sacred Codes of the Laws of the Universe. I cannot afford to indulge you with emotional upheaval, but I can explain to you in a loving way that there is a higher a purpose for you—and that is to deliver you into the sanctification of your own self-importance. The following paragraphs continue to explain the codes in a matter of physics, or Metaphysics.

May I begin to release the codes to you through the Collective Presence of Universal Love!

Your Notes:

CHAPTER TWO

Death Is Not An End—A Transition To A Different State Of Consciousness

Death—we are conscious one moment on the earth plane and a moment later we have passed over into the afterlife—there is a continuity of consciousness. We have transitioned into a different state of consciousness. When we die, we automatically return back to the source of all; and, through time as we know it here on the earth, we meld our mind, where we are able to facet our thoughts back into those whom we have left behind.

Through a Metaphysical interpretation consciousness during and after the dying process highlights the complexity and mystery of the fundamental aspect of life. That consciousness is not simply an individual phenomenon, but rather a collective one that is shared amongst humanity. From this perspective, the afterlife may be seen as a realm of consciousness that is shared by all who have passed on from this life. These are the Cosmic Codes of the Laws of the Universe/Collective Consciousness.

Within you, is a power, a consciousness—your life force—your Soul. Your Soul is your life's energy, your energy is your force field, and your force field is your aura, (the aura is the energy that is produced within your cells). Your Soul is the energy that collects from your unconscious/higher mind. We all have an individual consciousness and as we walk past one another, we feel it. Let us explore consciousness: Consciousness refers to an individual "sense of self" or "inner-self". An awareness of our own unique thoughts, sensations, memories, ideas, attitudes and beliefs. It is a sense of one's personal collective identity. Anything that we are aware of at any moment of time, forms part of our consciousness, and becomes our life force.

We have different levels of consciousness and each of us is able to access these levels as our intelligence evolves up into our hierarchical mind. A Metaphysically interpretation:

our brain has two hemispheres—two parts. The left-brain is our logic (conscious mind). The left-brain is our masculine side; our ego, our primal fear, and our logic. The right brain is our emotions (subconscious mind). The right brain is our feminine side, our inner creativity. We cannot survive on this planet without both ego and emotions. Our journey is to learn how to balance both brains so that we may advance our awareness of the supportiveness of our unconscious/higher mind or Higher Self (also known as the supra-consciousness, ultra consciousness etc.). The unconscious/higher mind is the freedom with which we can tune into ourselves, but only when the other two parts of our brain have balanced through our attitude to our self. Further information on the levels of consciousness can be found in Appendix D.

The mathematics of the Universe, which can be equated to pure energy, has always been here long before our gestation into human. This Universe and the millions of other Universes have always been in existence as a mathematical equation. In totality, it became the Divine Intervention or what we term as Natural Law; which we now refer to as the Collective Consciousness.

The Collective Consciousness inherits and creates the life force of every species that has inhabited the earth. Each species is autonomically connected through their inherited mind—or DNA—in order to review the life force of the previous generations. In humans, the information is embedded in our glandular (endocrine) systems; it filters through to the pineal gland, and then is absorbed into our DNA.

When the human foetus develops, the DNA of the foetus releases the embedded Universal energy, and an eternal soul life emerges (time variance occurs with every foetus). The energy of your Soul (aura) surrounds you; it is your life force. Your life is a miracle, it reflects the mirror of your cells out to others; therefore your light (your life force) is announced on a telepathic level-which becomes the co-creation of you. The foetus DNA is also the gathering of your forefathers and foremothers minds; this is also the life force of your DNA. Please remember that it is through the last strand of our DNA that we have continued to remain emotionally aware on this planet; it is that twelfth strand that we call "love", and it has the presence to hold all the other strands together.

Allow me to expand: Through the last strand of our DNA that we have continued to remain emotionally aware on this planet; it is that twelfth strand that we call "love", and it has the presence to hold all the other strands together. Through the codes of the Sacred Alphabet, the word "love" means "living the Oracle of life". If we bring the letter "i" into a circle, we have created the letter "o".

Metaphorically let us look at the word "aura", and then sound "aura-cle", which becomes the word "oracle", and then "ora", and then "cell". The aura is the energy that is produced within your cells; now you are aware that you are your own Oracle. This is through the manifestation of the reflection that ignites mathematically, through and from the chemicals adjusting throughout the neurons in the brain as you nurture back into yourself. Which means returning to self through accepting the intelligence you have earned. You are, after all, your own Alchemist.

Does the brain produce consciousness? The conscious-mind is already embedded in each cell of the human body. Every cell is a miracle into itself, that cell is a complete item of the Collective Consciousness. The brain is not the creature of consciousness it is one of the first multiplexes to evolve in the gestational period of consciousness. The brain re-wires itself by creating neural pathways to be compatible to the conscious-mind. It re-wires the conscious-mind as well as itself to exalt into a higher form of learning which is a higher level of consciousness. This automatically lifts us up to our next layer of intellect.

You exist and you are here through and for the benefit of mankind. You must learn to think before you do; and, more importantly, you must understand before you act. This thinking world of yours is called your "Essence", or your "Spiritual Self", and that self is here for you to realise the quest of your life.

On your life's journey, you will die to, and grow away, from your old ways of thinking. Through your own assertion, you will learn to release your fear through finding enough courage, strength, and power to believe that you are a miracle (a "mirror of your cell"). This is through you receiving a reflected image that is given back to you through the Eye of God.

What is God? God is the "Progressive Apostolate of the Collective Consciousness". This energy arranges us into a futuristic approach, where we deliver the miracles that we have earned back to the self. As we nourish ourselves from these Laws of God/Laws of the Universe/Collective Consciousness, we are allowed an expedient growth of worth, and this endows us to release and return the favours we have inherited. Only then do we have the ability to nurture others. It is a firmament of the heavens, which is represented to us firstly as the human brain. It is also reimbursed back to us through the scribing of the God Thoth, who, in Egyptian myth, measures our truth through the explanation of the hieroglyphs of Egypt. Through the evolution of the myth, Thoth is known to us as the "Architect" or the "Builder". When decoded, the word "mythology" becomes "my theology", which interprets to us as "my way of life".

What and how you are thinking right now is the result of what you have become up to this point; what you are doing on this journey of life is also learning to understand how you have been collected and created throughout your tribal laws, which are your generational families, in regards to how you have evolved from where they have come from. Remember as you move forward in a progressive way, you are automatically opening up your past generations experiences and clearing their karmic reactions which automatically rearranges the mathematical laws of consciousness. The abilities and opportunities you have understood so far will determine where you can go on to complete your journey of self-discovery.

While you are living this journey you are also in a process of dying, and, from death, a new life begins – it is a continuous cycle. No matter what thought you have in your mind, your energy travels around inside your aura and must always reconnect back to the beginning of its source, before you have completed the thought. This then allows the thought to release back into the Collective Consciousness through the complement you are receiving from your inner self.

When your intellect or your unconscious/higher mind is ready to separate from your body, death becomes imminent. It can take days, weeks, or years before your matrix collects and is measured through equalizing your mathematics back into its original source. The outcome of this—whether simple or complex—will all depend on your own intellectual belief.

Why the difference in time for this process? Some people retain a semiconscious connection with the body, through the remaining threads of ego or fear, once the Soul begins to release. Our fear, which we have inherited and systematically created, is hanging on through our lack of trust or belief in self. Fear will continue to remain caught up in the body, until we can feel the freedom of our thoughts associated with this word trust, and then, when we come to the point of acceptance, the fear will appear to disentangle and release itself. This occurs through you revisiting the experiences of your life's moments, after which time, the Soul is free to go on to its next Collective Inheritance.

Is this why we have this three-day sentience for the Soul to release? Has this idea come from Matthew 27:63, when the Pharisees said to Pilate, "Sir, we remember that the deceiver (Jesus) said while he was yet alive; after three days I will rise again." The number three (3), in Sacred Numerology, represents the Collective Mind/Consciousness. Can you see how we first began to unravel and understand the codes?

Your Notes:

CHAPTER THREE

My Late Husband

I watched as my late husband feared going into a coma prior to his death. He was afraid to let go of what he had always known himself to be, and he panicked at the thought of stepping into a world that, through his innocence, was unknown to his ego. He became very restless, as he did not understand where his unconscious/higher mind was leading him. It was waiting for him in the birthplace of his wings, which is the section of the body that surrounds the heart area, and which is also where the emotional feelings of "love" are born.

He had to connect back to the Metaphysical second-dimensional Mind of God; we know this as "AN", which is our inner university, the place where our feelings learn to balance. In other words, it is where we finally begin to trust and accept our self—where we harmonize our thoughts through the feelings of "love". It is the next stage of connecting us back into the original source. He had to come "home to himself" before he could let go and find a sense of peace within himself.

Once my husband was cradled in the arms of God and felt protected, he allowed himself to step into his coma, as he could no longer willingly create any excuses. He was then free to explore and go beyond his own boundaries, which allowed him to adjust and release the fear that he had created through his innocence to the unknown. I had to remain silent and still, and I communicated with him gently through both his and my unconscious/higher minds. I had become his life jacket as he thrashed about in his own stormy ocean. His passing was gentle and peaceful with our children present, as I was overseas, and I knew that he had finally accepted his next evolutionary step.

After his death, I found that, as I walked around during the day thinking my thoughts, I would feel my husband agree with something that I had collated within myself. It was as if he were in the same room as I was. I became quickly aware that, through the levels of my intelligence, his energy could easily tune into mine. I appeared as a safety valve, so to speak, for him to be free to adjust his thoughts. This was a profound revelation to me. Finally, I had to accept the offer that he felt he was contributing to my own thinking. He wanted me to find his late mother's certificates from the Conservatorium of Music and give them to the children. She was the youngest woman ever to receive a cap and gown from the Conservatorium of Music in Sydney, and he had taken great pride in her achievements. Those were the thoughts that had not been finalized before his passing, and they needed his instant attention as he journeyed on to the other side.

We were married for forty-two years, and the threads of consciousness and emotional responses had grown collectively during all that time. I could hear his thinking, in his innocence, as he adjusted to his new frequency. Once he trusted and accepted his release, he moved on. He has been a very good teacher in my search to understand death. The word "death", interpreted through the codes, means "the Divine 'EA' of the Truth of Heaven". During our marriage, we had many different experiences. Sometimes we worked and laughed our way through things, and other times we shared difficulties in communicating with one another. I blamed him for the lack of communication between us, and he blamed me. I never took the time to look at my own shortcomings, as I was relying on him to overcome them for me.

As an essential part of my training, I have learned that the problems I created were my own responsibilities—my own mistakes—through my own lack of insecurity, not necessarily through his! He was a worthy opponent, and a worthy opponent is someone we look into, not at; only then does that person become our equal.

Over the years, many people have asked me, through their innocence, to explain this sentience—or sentence—that we call "death". Here is one of their questions, followed by my answer.

Question: As I sat silently by the bedside of my dying wife, I thought that I was only imagining a conversation that was going on between us. Can you explain what was really going on, please?

Answer: It is through our mind not chattering that we learn to release and open up into our silence; it is through our intelligence releasing itself that we are able to hear all. Your wife was being brought up into her unconscious/higher mind, preparing to release her Soul; she was treading lightly with thoughts running to and fro. You are also in this same frame of mind in your stillness; very quickly, you both reach the same wavelength, and your thoughts combine with one another. Metaphysically, you have become the same age emotionally. Yes, you were having a conversation with your wife, so I hope that you paid attention and listened to her thoughts.

For further information on the Metaphysical interpretations of "AN" (Ascending through Nourishing) and "EA" (Energizing the Ascension), please refer to Chapter 15: A Metaphysical Interpretation of the Egyptian Afterlife and the Interpretation of the Three Gods "EL", "AN", and "EA" through Mythology.

Your Notes:

CHAPTER FOUR

The Passing Of Family, Spouses And Others To Release The Soul's Energy

As stated previously, our Soul is our life's energy, our energy is our force field, and our force field is our aura. Our Soul is the energy that collects from our unconscious/higher mind; it purifies and grants us stability for every positive step that we take. As we birth through and unfold our intelligence, it sets the scene for the next phase of our life.

It takes one step to step out from the crowd—just one step!—but, through that single step, the transformation of the emotional self begins. Through inheriting our own belief in self, as a result of taking that step, we allow the next person to take the next step—and then a whole series of steps are created for all of humanity. The understanding and awareness of the "interconnectedness" of consciousness/Collective Consciousness and DNA will lead to a clearer knowledge of the human potential.

Let us take a look at those who have made their mark—or step—for us to follow: Copernicus, Plato, Da Vinci, Newton, Einstein, Freud, Jung, and the list goes on and on and on. They stepped into themselves and searched; and then they stepped out from the crowd and up into the higher realm. All this was in order for the rest of humanity to step forward, as these great ones all had accomplished the levels of their Soul's intelligence. We are still using their examples to this day.

In some cases members of our family, spouse etc., pass over in order for us to move up into the next advancement of our inner-educated intelligence. On a metaphysical level it is a matter of energy as the Soul's journey is through the vibrational energy through our thoughts. This is the life force collecting.

My brother had to pass over in order to allow my first Shamanic teacher, who was an Aboriginal Elder with the Christian name of Peter, to enter into my life. I had to birth into my power, as my mathematics (energy of thoughts) had collected to allow my doorways or gates to be opened. I was trained in the ancient law through the family that Peter belonged to, which was the Pitjantjatjara tribe. Peter also died for me when my training through him was completed. He died through me reaching my emotional responsibility to self, which I did through his teachings. In-depth explanation in my book "Decoding the Shaman Within".

Exactly eighteen months after my brother's passing, and two weeks after Peter's, my younger sister, who was also age thirty-eight, also died for me. Not long after my precious sister's release, my beautiful father, who was also my first and greatest Spiritual teacher, died for me, too. He had to release for me as I had stepped up into my own higher realm; I had stood up and claimed my own power, and ninety days after my father died, my mother also died for me. My mother had to die through my evolving and accepting my higher emotional mind.

I had just lost most of my family in a short space of time, so understanding this information sent shock waves through me. I wandered, and wondered, over and over in my mind, what I had done to deserve this law of unconditional love. There was no way for me to go on other than to accept the pain that echoed through my heart—and also to acknowledge the glory of understanding and accepting this knowledge of truth and wisdom. I wanted to scream, "No! No!", over and over again, and it took me a long time to allow this collective offering to seat itself within me.

This Hidden God—"Ein Sof" (as it is spelt in today's language), "Ein Tzorph" (Aramaic)—as it is known throughout the Shamanic language; is waiting for us to release ourselves through our inner strength and belief. I like to think of it as the Collective of God. It was introducing itself to me in such a way that I had to learn, and also earn, my inner truth.

My family all died according to the Law of the Universe, in order that I had been exalted to move up into my next evolutionary step of intelligence. Through them passing over for me, I began to understand that there was a greater plan for humanity that I had not understood before. I watched as, over the next few years, I received the scars that my siblings had earned while they were here on the earth. Where did they come from? How did this occur? Somehow, the threads of their consciousness became a part of me! Had I earned them?

Over the previous twenty years, I had to walk the path slowly in order for those codes to be released inside me; I realized that I had surpassed my family through taking on the responsibility of understanding my next shift of consciousness. I was learning to master myself, and I became my own matrix through my intelligence equalizing to the matrix of what God/Collective Consciousness is.

If we understand the sacred codes on an inner Spiritual aspect, all we have to do is allow and accept the changes to our thinking, and then we can learn to apply resilience to our mind. Through this understanding, we give our children the freedom to ark their intelligence; to manifest their own time and space. This is the cohesive science of God; it is how the Laws of the Universe collect together. We attract these levels of higher intelligence, which are autonomically embedded in our cells, to us through the understanding of our left brain as it equates its own intelligence in order to become an added value to itself and also to harmonize with our right brain.

When one of our children makes a move forward, through accepting and equalizing the strength and power of his/her own intuition, he/she creates a mirror or reflection of our level. In other words, we release for them, so that they may inherit their next conciliatory appeasement. This release means that we must move our thinking forward; we must reconnect back to ourselves and rebalance our thinking in order for us to detach emotionally. This allows our children to become and believe in their own "hierarchical mind" (higher mind).

While we are hooked in to them emotionally, we feel a sense of responsibility for them, and they, in turn, feel responsible for us. Energy attracts attention. This attitude, in turn, deters both them and us from our own growth, and it also becomes a form of control—and this is not love. We can still love them and leave them, in order for us to get back in touch with our own lives.

These are a few of the secrets of the Hidden God/our Higher Self within, in regard to why so many people have to die. We are still innocently blundering our way through evolution. We each have our own ideas on what death is; I hope that this next step will explain and confirm my ideas to you even further.

When one of you steps before me for consultation, your families who are still here, as well as the evolution of your DNA and those who have already passed over appear, all stand behind you. Although they have physically passed over, they are still permanently in the Collective Consciousness. Why? Through the fourth-dimensional thought form. Another explanation is that the results of your unconscious/higher mind are free to release to me. This is the genetic inheritance of your DNA. As you were, so you shall live. Their previous experiences become your experiences, and the responsibility through all of this knowing, thus becomes yours. You are the channel for their success, and this then gives you the mind's right to evolve and expedite your own future.

Passing of My Brother and His Friends

My younger brother, Ray, who had passed over for my journey, came to me on the night before my father passed. With him stood two other men whom I recognized as James and Danny—they were his best friends during his lifetime. I looked at the three of them and said to Ray, "What are you doing here with those two?" He said, "Dad is coming home from hospital tomorrow." I said, "Yes, I know. I am going out there in the morning to stay a few days." I was on my way out west to where my family lived. Then I said to James and Danny, "What are you doing here with Ray? Have you met up with one another on the astral plane?" They looked at one another and said, "What?" And then both of them disappeared. Ray smiled at me and said, "I'll be back at a later time. I have a few things that have to be tidied up.". What he had to tidy up in heaven was not my concern. At that time of my training, I thought that my brother had reflected back to me what his earthly mind had remembered emotionally of his past. More to the point, I wondered why both of his friends had disappeared so quickly.

I had difficulty understanding why the three of them were together. I was so shocked at seeing Ray's friends James and Danny standing there with him that I went to the phone. We had all moved on over the years, and the old numbers were no longer applicable. I had to trace their phone numbers, as I had not communicated with James's family for many years, and I finally rang his wife. After the pleasantries were over, I said, "Please don't be upset, Jane, but I have had a vision. Ray came to see me!" I told her that I was puzzled because James and Danny had been with him. "What are you talking about?" she said. "James had an accident on the tractor and died nearly three weeks after Ray.". She then told me that Danny, who had been devastated about Ray's death, had died of a heart attack seven days after James. All had occurred with the code of 4 x 7 =28 days. So the three dear friends had all gone over, one right after the other. My father passed over early the following morning, so my brother Ray was right when he said, "Dad is coming home tomorrow."

When all this happened, my sister-in-law, Ray's wife, had just made a decision to take more of an interest in her own life; her educational fields began knocking at her door, and that opportunity gave her the chance to advance her life. Her children had grown and were heading out to conquer their own worlds; they were releasing themselves from her, so she had the chance to think over what she wanted to achieve for herself. At the same time, I was making the same decision to take control of my own life. Those two force fields opened up into the etheric winds and energized the doorway that we now understand as "unconditional love", and, through that, my brother was able to release himself. We had overstepped his mark. I was then able to see the threads coming together and connecting, as, 2,000 kilometres away, Jane had also made her decision to change her life. She was about to open her own clinic, so James had surrendered to the winds of change. Notice the codes in the numbers. Two represents the relationship of the Soul mind (Sacred Numerology).

Meanwhile, 4,000 kilometres away, Danny's wife was also changing her mind. She had just been offered a big promotion at work, and that meant moving to a new area thousands of miles away, so she was trying to work out how to tell her husband. Do you understand all this so far? Four represents the temple mind of the Soul. It was the end of the three deaths. Can you see through the layers of confinement that we place upon ourselves—and through the restrictions with which we bind ourselves?

It was not in the belief of others, it was the pureness of the belief, that those women had in themselves at that time; in other words, they had stood up in their belief and were being mathematically counted through the Universal Laws. Their intelligence had introduced them to their next opportunity, and they had surpassed their partners. It was through an ending of one existence to begin the next, which was correlated through a higher consultation (unconsciously) that each partner had with the other. The roles were reversing; the women were taking over a higher responsibility than their men.

Those three men had a perfect relationship with one another throughout their lives. As their friendship had grown through their respect of their own inner Higher Self viewing one another, they had, through their grieving process, become as one. One could not live without the other. When they had innocently suffered through the death of my brother, James and Danny had opened up their life program. Their wives had intellectually, in the moment, grown beyond them. Even to this day, their friendship with one another on the other side is still a respected state of grace. They often come in for a chat. This story is so similar to hundreds that I have listened to; when my clients have come to ask me to explain death to them regarding this wonderful mystery, they have returned home after the consultation to make enquiries regarding their own families.

I would like to make a short reference here to another learning I received through watching the Olympic Games. I have watched the last three Olympics in order to collect and gain my information regarding the education I was given.

The journey began when some athletes won their medals. Each person's life story emerged during the final gathering of their previous ninety-day period—that is, before the games. For one athlete to win that gold medal, his father had to pass over. For another athlete to win the silver medal, her mother, who had reached her own zenith, had to die for the sake of her next thought (her child.) For someone else to earn the bronze medal, it was usually a grandparent or a favourite uncle or aunt, who had succumbed for the sake of the athlete. Do you understand what I have just written?

It all depended on the Law of Attraction as to how the athletes' minds had collected on behalf of themselves. It was through their genuine belief and knowing that they were good enough, through their deliberation, to attract their final outcome. They had earned these medals. The mathematics had already decided on the outcome. It made no difference which sporting field they were representing; they had earned the specified ignition through their own forthrightness.

Energetic Fields of the Collective Consciousness

On 31 August 1997, Diana Princess of Wales released her Soul and passed over. The shock to humanity's thinking changed the molecular structure of the whole planet; we opened our hearts, through the emotional grief of the Collective that we all felt within, in regard the loss of a young woman who was so popular in our hearts and minds. These fields stayed open as we waited for the funeral of Diana; more than two billion people from around the world watched the ceremony on TV, all at the same time.

Through the emotional support that humanity shared with one another, we gave that wonderful woman, Mother Teresa, the opportunity to release herself to God. She passed over five days later, still during the gathering of the codes—through the mathematical procedure of seven days—after our hearts had opened for Diana. Mother Teresa's energy was so highly infused into the Divine Energy that she could not die of her own accord; through her having no family to inherit her intellect, she had to earn the freedom for her Soul to die. One tall mast opened the door for the other to enter!

The Princess of Wales was buried on the day following Mother Teresa's death. The change of the energetic fields of the Collective Consciousness opened up millions of doorways to advance humanity into releasing their inner feelings. Why? This was through humanity being so emotionally touched, which allowed the Collective Energy to spiral up to be absorbed into the Collective Inheritance of the Consciousness. The funeral service for Diana was held on 6 September, as stated previously one day after the passing of Mother Teresa, and was in its correct order for the energy of the Collective Consciousness to inherit itself. Our emotional energy morphs throughout the planet, and we are brought back to our own attention as part of the Collective, in order to rebalance the future inheritance of the planet as a whole. Therefore, we must face up to the responsibilities that we have forced ourselves to overlook.

CHAPTER FIVE

The Quantum Hologram—Why A Partner Dies For The Other Partner To Progress In The Journey Of Life

As we are about to die, the Soul expands its belief and slowly releases up autonomically into the next parallel world. It then learns to disentangle the strands that the ego—or fear—had wrapped around it, for support, throughout the physical body. Those energies then change and grow through their own enhancement, the gift that you are adhering to them. Your energy can never die; your antimatter can leave your matter. That antimatter is what we call "etheric energy"—or the electromagnetic energetic light waves—that vibrate and coerce with one another right throughout the Soul energy of the planet. This is your Spirituality at work.

The Quantum Hologram that is the creation of all of us is comprised of these electromagnetic waves that cohere until they become coherent, and then they have the opportunity to reform themselves. The higher and more powerful your vibrations become through accepting your intelligence and wisdom, the more your waves have the opportunity to become aware of their capability of separating—through which you will have the strength to regenerate the self. String theories are at work here, now read on!

Those threads of energy multiply and become your power force, where your arachnoid layer transforms into your Etheric Web—that is, the web of your Divine Consciousness, which is spread permanently out there, repeating itself throughout the Collective Consciousness, forevermore. Through the principles of Shamanism, we have named this experience "unconditional love". After death, these layers of love filter back down through your family.

Allow me to explain how we, the readers of these Cosmic fields, help you, our client. Those personalities that we readers see in our vision worlds, when we are in consultation with the unconscious/higher mind of our clients, are a hologram of the client's personalities—or emotions—that need attention in that moment. We readers mentally connect to this energy and we have the possibility of helping you, our client, to correct the flow of the personality (aspect of self) within, that you are not aligning yourself with. Usually, it is one that has been through an existence of you holding onto your suppressed emotional life.

Your personalities (aspects of self) are the added value of your characters that will always support you. This explains how the Asian languages have collected their characters to create their languages—from ancient cuneiform and hieroglyphs to the pictograms still used today— in order to explain the written word! It is like writing in instant shorthand. If we express the truth in a group of sentences, it is much easier to understand. The mind can create time in order to hear the complete story on an inner level.

The reason you have attracted someone from your past (i.e., aunts, uncles, cousins, grandparents, parents, siblings, friends, spouses, lovers, etc., in a reading) is through each or all of them reflecting in you a part of yourself that you and they had melded together through same mindedness. All the same family had similar genetics, which coerce to create your tribal/family inheritance. For friends, spouses, and/or lovers, the connection is different, but no less powerful. Do you understand? When in doubt please read the above paragraph again in order to reimburse what you are having difficulty in accepting and understanding; one day, you will read it, and there it is—total understanding! It took me years of going over it, again and again, to bring it together in the first place!

This is how we tune in and gather our respect for one another; we become friends when our thoughts have registered with theirs, and, when we die, that emotion also stays in an energy field that we can comply with. This is the "Quantum of our own personal Hologram" resetting our life scene. These aspects—or facets—of Divine Consciousness await our proprietary earnings (energy of our thoughts, feeling and emotions). Those feelings or emotions are recorded into our memory banks—and remain there for the rest of our life.

Here is another example. A woman whose husband had just passed over came to see me. They had lived together for many years and had shared many sexual experiences; in the process, they had built an etheric eclectic field between themselves. As such, they had gained a "religious" experience with one another over the years. The reason I bring sexuality in at this time is through the substantial foundation of how feelings grow and connect between life partners. This is why we search for a relationship: to satisfy our ego, which it is afraid to face life on its own. It is a natural urge for the ego to feel it needs company to support its thinking; as it meets with others, it is searching for a compatible mind to ark itself to. This ark becomes the ego's light, which alters the characters of each personality, and that, in turn, reflects inside the self!

Therefore, the lives that they shared and created together must now separate—and, through time, this will take around twenty-four months, at which point, her yearnings will rethread themselves into other areas. Why twenty-four months? Her DNA of twenty-four strands, which create the double helix, must now vibrate into a different frequency to allow her to adjust, through her thoughts returning to her past regarding what they had shared together. The more we dwell on the past, the longer it takes to equate. The more we respect the experiences of the past, the freer the mind becomes to release the depth of the past.

They had been married for thirty-four years. The number thirty-four (34), in Sacred Numerology, is denoted as "my mind is my temple". Her husband had to submit his temple to hers and die, as she had allowed herself to do what he was too afraid to do. He was waiting for his retirement; he was shutting himself down. She had finished with the child-rearing and knew that the grandchildren were the responsibility of her own children, so she was earning her freedom to nurture her own desires.

That woman had chosen to step up into the next level of her intelligence and rediscover her education; she had chosen to stand in her own strength, and so her husband had to submit his. She had moved beyond him mentally and emotionally. He had released his life for her in pure unconditional love. When the happiness in the relationship has outgrown its moment of distinction, it becomes a hard lesson for most of us to accept.

When we give ourselves to someone in marriage and share a sexual temple (higher mind) liaison, we meld a parallel world of our thinking. We come together, and, when the restrictions of our bondage have lifted, the intuition of our self returns back home to reignite the word "yearning", where we begin to step forward and look for the next experience to inherit. No future exists for any one of us as long as we keep on living and creating excuses that we have already earned.

It is only when we mentally step out of the world that we have shared with one another—and I mean "mentally"—that we realize we can no longer find the answer to relive our old excuses. So we turn away from the mundane existence of our marriage, and we look for answers through something else that will give us more self-satisfaction. We have outgrown the world we created together long ago. Again, it is to the detriment of self that the Laws of the Universe must return the results of our thinking back to us.

That woman came to see me, as she was not able to switch off and tuck away that thirty-four-year relationship. The shock of her husband dying, before she could realize the consequences of what had been created through her walking away mentally, had immediately brought her back to the world she had been living in and sharing with him. That relationship had been a part of her everlasting energy; it had been the pulse of her heartbeat. His world and her world and the parallel world that they had created with one another all had to separate from the threads that held them together.

This does not mean that she would forget those years of togetherness—we cannot do that; it is just not that simple. She now has to learn to rethink and reinstate herself in order to look at the relationship differently. She has to learn to look at it through the changes that she had made, through yearning for a more advanced acceptance of self. She had depended on him for so many years, and now she must work twice as hard and learn to reshape her thinking. Autonomically, through the collection of her own nervous system, she will allow herself time for her future opportunities to release those new changes, which, in turn, will step forward to present the next chapter of her life.

If we care to be honest with that statement, we will understand it by looking through the files of our own family history—where the truth is releasing itself. And that is what the woman had already achieved through her own countenance of facing up to herself.

Back to the Soul. Our Soul begins to gather and collect its web, and it departs from the body days before our death—or when the mind accrues into its own stabilization, in order to allow the body to slow down. Some Souls begin to bounce outside their body up to eight weeks or more before they die, although the program of their existence must be initiated and mathematically completed before they are allowed to leave the planet. There is never a mistake created through God's (Greatest Oracle of the Divine) eyes.

That woman's husband could not have left the planet until his wife had initiated her new train of thought to begin the next extension to her own program. That is the wisdom of the Laws of the Universe: for her to become her own Law of Self—the "law of her own universe".

You see, this is the truth that has been collected through the mathematics of the Universe, in regard to the word "love". Love is unconditional; it is explaining to us how we are all here to learn to live our Oracle of life. Love is absolute when it is delivered unto us (from above) through the collective of all. Unless we interfere with our own program for the sake of others, the program automatically becomes adherent. It has always been here to continue to give us each support. It's just that you were never aware of it before! Remember, everything that I am reminding you of is already instilled and embedded in your genes.

CHAPTER SIX

The Three Doorways—Three Stages Of Death

There are three stages of death for us to understand; I will explain them to you through my interpretation.

You have just been given a death sentence from the doctor, informing you of a dis-ease that has attracted its own free rein to overtake your body very quickly. The first stage of death begins with the shock of being told that you have been given the death sentence; we find that, very quickly, your ego disassociates itself from your emotions, as this information has completely stunned it! The ego doesn't know how to deal with this information, and it doesn't want to know!

<u>The number one (1) in Sacred Numerology represents "I am"</u>

This information equates through the conscious mind of self, which is the responsibility of the egotistical left brain, and, when it is in doubt, it turns to register its thoughts through to the subconscious mind—that is, the emotional right brain. Of course, it expects to pass on the responsibility of what it has created to someone else. This gives it freedom in the moment, and it thinks it can continue on in its merry way. That is why the ego has no continuation in its memory banks. It has difficulty holding onto a momentous thought, and the only way it can nourish itself is through relying on what has already been!

Your emotional mind collects these vibrations and converts them into feelings, which are flushed throughout your system, where they are automatically collected and brought up through to your pituitary gland—this is the doorway into the Divine energy, which is your unconscious/higher mind (Soul). This mind becomes aware of your inner emotional stutter, where your ego is beginning to lose its self-control. Your higher mind holds the energy of every cell in your body, and it hears your ego placing your thinking into the "too hard basket", uttering, "But what about me? I AM!" By using the word "but" in the beginning of your sentence, you have already begun to create your next excuse! The unconscious/ higher mind begins to coerce with the ego; and this is where your other senses begin to understand what it has created for itself.

Stage One of Death is for your ego to learn who you are, and then accept that you are about to head towards an end of the old experiences that it has contained for itself! The body is doing what comes naturally, and so this is where you have the opportunity to learn how to surrender to your self. Time will become the ego's teacher.

The liver begins to empty out its aggression, and it voluntarily tips into the gall bladder. When you are living out the thought processes of how you have lived your life—and when you are in doubt about it—you automatically pass yourself onto the next coherent moment.

<u>The number two (2) in Sacred Numerology represents "the relationship to self"</u>

When you reach your state of acceptance, Stage Two of Death begins to step forward into your psyche. In some people, this second stage can be a very bitter part of the game of death; it is a time when the channels of your thoughts open to remembering and releasing your past experiences back to you. It does not begin with the happier times. The ego will have a tendency to remind you of the bitterness that occurred throughout its life—when it could not get its own way—and it will automatically look for the shortcomings of all the experiences that were regaled upon you. It must learn to come back into the relationship of self.

This area is what we call the "gall energy", and the gall bladder is the organ—or "planet"—in your own "universe", where you store your toxic chemicals. It has the responsibility to filter the anger from your liver and collect the bitterness of the suspended fear that you have already created. The gall bladder now comes to its own realization: that it must cleanse this anger and purge itself before death. The memories that it has stored on your behalf must come to the surface, where you learn to face up to the responsibilities you have earned.

That bitterness is the ego being fed its own demise.

Sometimes, this can be the stage when you tell all those people, with whom you have never been truthful with, what you really think of them. It can be when you tell your partner about the disappointments that you have long stored away in your hidden pantry.

It is a time where you earn this surrender and bow to yourself. This respect filters back into your cells, and you are learning to see up and into—not just looking at yourself, but into your self—which assists all your feelings to want to redeem the hidden freedom that has been trapped by your ego throughout your lifetime.

The rest of your internal organs now have the opportunity to begin their own cleansing process; they are the collectors of your co-existence. This is where we begin to accept the concordance of self. They must be adhered to, as this sets the patterns for the Divinity of death to congratulate itself.

Look back at those you have loved—those who have died for you—and, in your own truth, you will remember what emotions they went through as they learned to accept their own destiny. I refer to Stage Two as the blame stage, where you empty your own cup by releasing the thoughts about why you blamed others for your own shortcomings. Once that is done, you have the opportunity to blame and reflect to yourself. You are entering back into your own educational university, where you are being reminded of your own shortcomings so that you can reshape your mind in order to begin again.

This is where we, as therapists, have the opportunity to come in and remind you that you now have the opportunity to construe your thinking; you will now be able to reinvest in your self before the scales have tipped into their abundance. Your shock has been realized, and, when you come home to self-realization, you certainly have the opportunity to regenerate and begin again. The ego has sustained itself and is ready to listen. In other words, very simply, you have learned to surrender to "you".

If not, the story continues into Stage Three.

<u>The number three (3) in Sacred Numerology represents "the mind"</u>

Stage Three is the final stage of Death. This is where you are free to remind yourself that you have accepted death—that you are ready to surrender your greatest gift to God. This is where the ego submits, and you turn your life over. Stage Three occurs through your acceptance; you can willingly accept the inner freedom that the Soul releases. Through the language of the Shamanic Inheritance, it is the "applause we return to God".

Many people have released from the body in my arms. In most cases, their final words were, "Oh! Look at the colours!" They each died with a smile on their faces. As death occurs, your energy moves up into the Collective Mind (the higher mind); this has opened up on your behalf and prepared a balanced mind for you prior to this moment. These colours are free to release, once your ego submits to your emotions, and they become the rainbow which naturally harmonizes the body in preparation for the passing from one world to the next. The exchange of energy becomes easier through the mathematics arching throughout the body. Again, Einstein comes to mind through his explanation of the fields of relativity through time and space. We know that this creates gravity, so, in order for us to release our fields of gravity, we become eremitical—that is, the Soul absorbs our energy to bring us home to God. The more intellectually (emotionally) reformed you are, the easier the changeover.

There is no set time frame for those three stages, and not everyone goes through them in the same order (although the order of Stages One, Two, and Three as I have described them is the most typical). It depends entirely on how that person has lived up to their intelligence, and how he/she has accepted the merits of inner wisdom prior to death.

For example, when my husband passed on, I saw him go through only two stages; he exhibited no anger or animosity. He had released his anger in the years before he died, so by the time he came through the second stage, he had already said all the things that he had wanted to say. Death came quickly for him; he had simply had enough. When the Soul finally releases from the body, your fear must then face and surrender to itself—quite simply, there is no one left to argue with.

The Soul cannot become trapped in the physical body; the body cannot surrender fully until the Soul has collected the life force and is ready to leave. It is only the last of the old fear that we have already created, through the innocence of our own belief, that is left in the body—and, it is those last remaining threads of our fear that keep us aware of our momentary surroundings.

The Soul is well above the body before the body stops breathing, so death is painless. It waits for the ego. Someone always comes to help us leave our layered garments (our body) behind—before we cross to the other side—always remember, we are never left to make the journey alone. If someone crosses over through the result of an accident, the ego—or fear of self—often echoes back through that person, until he/she can accept being in another dimension of time. The cause of his/her actions must release throughout the scrolls of adjustment, which allows the memory to free itself. Such individuals do not carry on, day after day, in pain as many of you think. Always remember that, when someone comes through with this announcement, the message is for that person—it is certainly not a message carried for the one who has departed. The pain must be eradicated before the Soul can leave. (Note that suicide is explained in its own chapter, not here.)

Your Notes:

CHAPTER SEVEN

The Passing To The Afterlife

We refer to the "afterlife" by many other names: "dimensional time-shifting", "cellular recognition", "Heaven", "other side", "holographic imprints", and "parallel worlds". The speed at which those who have passed over understand what has happened to them all depends on their belief in their emotional self, which is now the accumulation of their intellect.

Let us take the passing of a grandmother as an example. She had lived her life to its zenith, and God stepped in to allow the next positive equation from her tribe to inherit the kingdom of the family. While we are mourning her passing, the grandmother is releasing herself into a parallel world. She remains in the Collective Consciousness of the planet after passing over, and she is busy transferring herself to the evolutionary level that she has equated with the Collective. All her old thoughts are there with her—her life, her dreams, her logic thinking (i.e., her everyday existence). And she now has the opportunity to sift through the layers of her mind, which she has collected for her own security, and sort herself out. The most astounding thing that she first begins to realize is that her body feels free! There is no pain, no heaviness, no darkness—and she becomes enlightened. She is now on her alternative pathway, where she "alters the old native" within! This parallel planet becomes her new home; through the emotional processing of her time spent here, her energy will connect back to her own DNA, where she becomes reconnected to her original tribe/family.

On the "other side", she is learning to understand how she can connect with the Collective Consciousness. Her photographic memory is busily working through her conscious and subconscious energy, where she is releasing her memories up into her unconscious/higher mind, and this is how we Shamans have the opportunity to listen to her thoughts. In her childlike way, the grandmother has begun to live again; but, first, she is free to revisit each memory of her life and enjoy the experience of doing her "ethereal" quest in the first few weeks after her death. After that, the threads of the grandmother's own consciousness reward her back into the Kingdom of God, and, through her own attainment, she returns back home.

I remember my own journey with the passing of my parents and siblings, all of whom echoed their thoughts back to me as they learned to understand what was happening to them. Some explain this as "going into the light". The "light" is your future intelligence reflecting back to you all the possibilities of your inheritance.

An "old Soul" is a Soul that is full of the past inheritance of the forefathers and foremothers. Old Souls have all the knowing of the mind, but the fear that was instilled in the previous generations can be re-created very quickly in the given moment. An old Soul carries the fear of the past generations through its DNA, and then it sits back to watch and learn through its own silent wisdom.

In contrast, "new Soul" is an innocent Soul. A new Soul has no fear; it walks along innocently. The old Soul is "in-no-sense", and the new Soul is "innocence". One is the adult, and the other is the child—yesterday and today, old and new.

CHAPTER EIGHT

The Transformational Process

When family members have passed over and reached the next dimension, they begin the transformational process. Their thoughts multiply through the Collective Consciousness, as they learn to equalize their mind, and carry themselves forward into the oneness. This is where thought attracts thought, energy attracts energy, time attracts time, and attention springs to attention. They begin to mirror their intelligence back into their reflective light as they enhance their freedom through the expediency they are earning.

For example, a member of your family dies. Five days later, Mrs Smith from down the road comes up to you and says, "Your Bill came and saw me last night; he must have arrived safely, as it didn't take him too long to come back."

It is Bill's positive thinking in the hereafter that sparks his energy vibrations back here to the planet. He could return through Mrs Smith, as she was sufficiently balanced in her mind to hear him. Because you were still in the grieving process, you could not hear him. When we spend our time grieving, our energy becomes heavier, and we miss the transformation process of helping our loved ones adjust into their new abode.

In consciousness, when we die, we automatically return back to the source of all; and, through time as we know it here on the earth, we meld our mind, where we are able to facet our thoughts back into those whom we have left behind. Bill, through his expediency, has accepted each step of freedom, as a result his own mathematics adjust to his own request—which explains how quickly his time has released him back to where the feelings of his heart still feel at home.

Dreams are created through your unconscious/higher mind communicating back to you; they are reminding you of the lessons that you need to understand regarding yourself. You cannot hear them if your mind is filled with incessant chatter. The ego refuses to conform when it is in control of the moment. A Shaman is trained to open up the psyche and live in the waking dream state of consciousness, which is an added extension to the world of truth. Dreams can range from a pleasant dream, which could be a recommendation to add to what you are doing, to a nightmare, which is a wake-up call from your God/Higher Self within regarding what you are doing to yourself. Your Higher Self is asking you to please rectify your thoughts before they mass together!

Your Notes:

CHAPTER NINE

Death: Accidents, Young Children, Your Thoughts

Now we move on to discuss when people are taken abruptly through an accident; they are also living the mathematical program of the inheritance of their family. Over and above that accident is the occident, and the occident is how they created that accident through their mathematics being realigned to their thinking. The occident is another way to explain the Laws of the Universe in action. The mathematical codes have clicked into action and been brought together! Go back to the conversations you had with this wonderful person who has passed over under this type of circumstance—and please remember that he/she had been aware of the changes in their life three days prior to passing over.

If only we all could understand this area more collectively, we would begin to realize that our thinking is our foremost priority—it is what allows us to theorize and release the Soul's evolution for the whole family tribe. This is also instigated throughout the whole of humanity; we set the wheels in motion not only for our own family, but also for the town or village that we live in. After which, it ventures out to the state, and then to the whole country, and we are obliquely designing how many deaths will occur for all humanity to bear. We are oblivious to the consequences of our own thinking, and yet, all the time, the mathematics (energy) of the Collective Consciousness still keeps adding up our thoughts.

Please remember that someone always comes to help before we cross to the other side; we are never left to make the journey alone even in the case of accidents.

When young children die, we find that they can surrender very simply; they can accept their passing quite easily. The predicament begins to create itself when we, as parents, start mentally trying to call them back to us. We have had full responsibility of caring for and rearing this child, and it is quite natural for us to want to know where our child is going.

Yes, we know our little one is journeying into heaven, and yes, we also know our little one is placed in God's arms. Now add this information to your own portfolio, the children are well protected by the young beings of light who care and play with them as they grow up into their maturity of intelligence. Also don't forget the Grandmothers and Grandfathers who shower them with love and cuddles, which gives the child their own sustenance in regards to a family life. Through our innocence, we want to be with our child; and, somewhere deep inside our thinking, we believe that our child has been cut short of his/her own existence. However, this is not so, as I can assure you having listened to hundreds of families release their stories through the experience of losing their child.

First, we initiate our loneliness, and this sets off a chain of emotional personalities of self (aspects of self), which try to add themselves up through their lack of understanding this higher realm. We are told by some that "God has a plan for us" or that "it was meant to be". We are also told that we must not question God! Well, I did! What was this guilt that I was feeling for having been robbed by God? Was this created through the ego yearning for its own demeanours? We have a name for this emotional personality that keeps on popping up its head: grieving. The cry arises from deep within us, "Why did this happen to my child—and, what about me?"

The ego has to walk back into and through the mind in order to collect itself. If we can adhere to that, it frees the child and allows his/her hierarchical (higher) mind to be endowed into the garments of God. In order for us to release those thoughts and words of guilt and grief, we must raise ourselves higher. When we note the changes in our thinking, we open up into the emotional kingdoms of our love and freedom. We have named this respect, and this earns its way into our Soul. It takes time for us to let go—and I say this to you through the echo of my own heart being educated into its higher realms.

Many people have told me that they can feel their child around them after he/she has passed over. They may well feel that, but the child is not there to contact the parent, unless the child has something to say. Remember that, for the Soul to release, all must be mathematically equated correctly. Learn to still your mind and listen—you will see whether it is you calling for your child, or your child calling you. The child usually calls to inform you to stop grieving and get on with your life. Usually, those are the first words they speak when they have made contact with us. The realm that they have stepped into is full of rainbows and colours that you are not even aware of yet. Stop feeling guilty! Allow the mathematics to accrue, through the gift that you have been given by your child, in order to become dignified in your recognition of self.

That child's new position is to evolve through his/her own freedom, in order to continue into the next informative step of intelligence—that new position is not for the child to hang around here. In this new realm, the child will continue learning through accepting the next teachings and beginning the next education. They still grow up through the Soul's afterlife. Stop feeling sorry for yourself. That child died for you; please realize that your child gave you the greatest gift of love—where it became a spark of light, and that came to us from God's love. No, humanity does not yet understand the truth regarding love through the strength of God, but these lessons are on their way. Hopefully, now we can accept these Laws of the Universe, and, through that acceptance, we can change the world for the better and for all of humanity to view.

I have asked these parents, "What were your thoughts creating for you, through your own lives, before your child's passing?" With the greatest respect, I have also asked, "How did you, as the parents, set the ball rolling?"

That is, how did the eclectic experience shape up to itself, through the Oracle of the lives of the parents—and their child—being brought together? Yes, I can be kind and mention that God had a purpose for this child to be given to you for a brief experience to show you the way. That doesn't really answer your questions though, does it? Now, please allow me to explain to you how you can enter into the kingdom of mathematics, which becomes the religion of science; or, is it the other way around, where it becomes the science of religion? There are two heavenly realms of intelligence here that must harmonize with one another in order to bring the balance that will allow the next generation of your tribal family to inherit their freedom—all through their responsibilities to themselves.

When a child is released into the heavenly realms before his/her seventh year, he/she has accrued, through the DNA of the family law, taking on the parents' responsibility—that is, the responsibility that you, the parents, innocently have not been able to view for yourselves.

A child dies through either parent's not having accepted the responsibility of him/herself, and who finds him/herself hesitant towards taking the next positive step. Those parents are not listening to the worthiness of their own thoughts that have been gathering over time. Your family/tribes are all measured through the mathematics of the Laws of the Universe.

A "son" dies for our left brain—our ego—or the strength that we have not allowed ourselves to become. A "daughter" dies for our right brain—our inner creativeness—or our own emotional responses that we cannot believe and trust in as yet. Those children are the results of our future generation, which is the development of our next thought. Once the child has gone through into the Collective Consciousness, he/she becomes a treasure trove for all humanity to look up to.

I realize that this story may sound cold and calculating to a few of you, although, through twenty years of speaking to thousands of you who have lost a child, I still must go on and explain the hidden truth. Many of you became affronted at my words in the beginning of our seminars or private consultancy. However, as I continued to explain these hidden laws to you, through the layers of the metaphorical wisdom releasing itself as to how you memorized your thoughts through the past three or four generations, you had the opportunity to revise your thinking when the truth revealed itself to you. That truth is released through the understanding of the mathematics of the family mind, which is the collection of your DNA combining with the Collective works—or words—of God. Do you see the advantages of the gift that our children leave behind for us to inherit when they die so young?

Let us understand and accept this Law of the Universe in all its glory, and let us stop making excuses for our own fear, which has not, as yet, discovered its own freedom. That fear is still trapped in our ego, which is the innocence of the child within. Hopefully, through you understanding my words, you will go on to explain to others that these keys were brought forth through the gestation, and they are permanently endowed with the same knowledge. I thank you and bless you for reading through these paragraphs.

Your Notes:

CHAPTER TEN

When an Elderly Life Partner Dies

When an elderly life partner dies, the responsibility is then placed on the one who is left behind. The couple has been eating, sleeping, walking, and talking together for over fifty years, and, over that time, the temple that created their relationship has become as one. Which one of the two had the most Spiritual connection to themselves? The mathematics have been adjusted according to their laws for one of them to release. Look back to your own parents or grandparents to see which one had the most inner strength. Look to see which one surrendered, in order for the other to continue on so that they could learn to earn their next educational (emotional intelligence) step.

My father had the most inner strength, and that is why he had chosen to die first. After my father passed over, my mother had to face up to her own difficulties. She did so, and this was through the relationship of her own acceptance as to how she had respected herself. She lived for my father, and was always on standby to serve him. I watched her grow in her wisdom as she had to face herself alone; the more she accepted herself, the more my love for her deepened.

An elderly parent cannot die while they are waiting for their children to grow up to overtake them. If it is the mother who is suffering, she cannot release until her child has birthed the strength of his/her emotional mind. If it is the father who is still alive, he must wait for the strength of the child to equalize him logically before he is free to return home. When you are in the empowerment of the Collective Consciousness, the first step to accepting this information is that your parents must release for you.

The opportunity for them to stay here is also available, but only if they have the inner strength to detach emotionally from the family. If they can do this, they will be able to collect their worship back to themselves, and then they are free to go on with the discovery of accepting their new life. What can elderly parents do when they feel that they have reached their own zenith? Where can they go? They must release all their past thinking to be able to change into their next powerful thought. More importantly, they need to take more control of their own life and stop trying to control the rest of the family or hold them emotionally at bay. A new beginning is always through an acceptance of adding more responsibility to self. By accepting this inner strength of self, you become more intellectually enlightened, and this source of light is you living in heaven while you are still right here on the earth.

When a member of our family dies for us, we can learn to look at whether that death is for the past or the future. Our children represent our future, and our parents represent our past. Our parents relate to what we have already overcome, and our children relate to what we have the opportunity to become. If your parents are elderly and still alive, there are changes that you must make in your own consciousness. In your own time, you will develop these paragraphs and learn to understand these laws.

I have been inundated with elderly people asking me questions, such as: "Why am I still here?" "Why can't I die?" "Why will God not take me?" The most important one that they ask is when they reach towards me and say, "I have had enough. I have reared my children, and now they have theirs. I have lived my life, so what do I have to do before I die?" Gently, I coerce them into the teachings about how their family must birth their own intelligence and evolve before the parent can return home (pass over). Most of them are proud to take on the role of the Adept, and they are willing to find the courage and accept the challenge that is set before them. They now have time to rethink and understand their family, which turns to a deep love and respect for who they are as human beings.

There is a tribal family web that we weave, and the message comes through to those who have changed their opinion of themselves and extended an invitation, through the family law, to climb up their own ladder of success. I have already explained your parents and your children. Allow me to explain the rest of the family tribe that you belong to.

Your brothers and sisters are equivalent to what, why, and who you are becoming. They represent a close personality of self in regard to how your mind is harmonizing and preparing your moment.

A cousin, aunt, or uncle represents a distant thought of yours that has not yet come into its own fruition. One of them is helping to prepare the future for you.

Grandparents are a precious thought, and they have earned their stay through the second generation. They are the higher mind—or the overlords—of the family, and their task is to equate the lineage. Doors of consciousness open wider and more easily for them, and they find that new experiences are available to them, right at their fingertips.

Your Notes:

CHAPTER ELEVEN

Interacting with the Soul

It has taken us a few years to come to terms with the intelligence of the unconscious/higher mind. We have always been aware of it, but we didn't quite understand it. We are becoming more aware of its intellect as we open up our own intelligence with each positive inner step we take. The unconscious/higher mind is communicating through us, twenty-four hours a day, and, slowly, we are becoming aware of the language of how it communicates back to us. If we ignore this sensory perception, the laws collect, and we find that the next weakest member of our family tribe will have to pay the price for our thoughts; or, through our ignorance, we earn the right to collect the dis-ease that is created on behalf of our thinking.

The brain communicates to us only through this telepathic inheritance, which is the hidden language of the unconscious/higher mind. It mathematically relays each message, which, collectively, is relayed through our thinking. (References to this inner wisdom are also explained to you in my book, "Decoding Dis-ease".)

Even we who have been trained in these fields are still retraining our own thinking into accepting these worlds that we now live in momentarily in our existence. The most important order of your life is right here and now. This thought that you are reading is the most important in your existence. It does not matter to me whether the person is alive or dead; I live totally with and through the vibrational inheritance of my unconscious/higher mind. I was educated and trained for a number of years to read that energy, through my mind being trained and exfoliated to evolve up into the quantum holographic resonance. When a voice asks me a question, I am available to give an answer, through us both reaching the same resonance of same mind.

Children have a much better view of death than most adults do. This is all through the reasoning that children are still connected to their inner truth, so they feel that it is quite okay for them to die. Deep within them is instilled the knowing of the mathematics, which construe to the unconscious/higher mind.

Hospitals realize the instant benefit of the life-support system, where, in the given moment, they can help a patient remember their service to themselves—although I would like you to think about this next equation, as, when this continues over a long period of time, it is time for you to rethink your thoughts! When someone is put onto a life-support machine to postpone death, that machine takes over to extend that person's life force. While we are keeping someone alive against his/her Divine will, it interferes with the next step of the family's emotional inheritance. I would like to add another response, too—we are interfering with the quality of life that the next generation will intellectually inherit. Go back over the previous paragraphs, please, and reaffirm to yourself just what it is that you are interacting with.

Your Notes:

CHAPTER TWELVE
Death is of Your Design

Let us take a journey into the unconscious/higher mind, where we go beyond the worlds of emotion to see how we promote death through our thinking. Death is of your own design; it is a sacrament that is constantly programming itself between you and God, this amazing Greatest Oracle of the Divine. There is a program for every human on this planet, and that program must be adhered to and fulfilled; it must be fulfilled through the codes that represent the mathematics of your Soul. This repetition is repeated over and over again until humanity, as a whole, starts to accept the system to move beyond their priority moment.

Let me explain your life program to you. I conduct many business seminars around the planet, and I explain this story to all of them. A company sells a product which proved to be a success in their own country, so they wish to go international. They employ people to take on the responsibility showing that product to other countries. The design of the product is now on the move, and, through confidence, this product is sold to countries of similar mind. They place their orders, and, through their confidence in the product, they show it to others, and then it goes on to branch out to more of same mind. This builds up through a positive action of confidence in the product.

As this energy collects itself and grows, the original company gets an order from a country that has heard of the product but has not yet had the opportunity to see it. Isn't this the dream of every business? The product takes over and begins to sell itself! Do you see how the energy is returning back to its original source? The business is now setting a system of success which is working on its own behalf. Instead of you working for the company, the company steps up to the next level of thinking, where the next product is brought out on to the drawing board.

To further explain, the previous example is the same Metaphysical interpretation of your life program. Your life program was created through your parents' DNA, which provided the basic principles for you to become you. Your task is to unfold yourself through the disadvantages of your parents' judgment and (mis)understanding themselves! You have chosen to live what your parents were too afraid to face through their acceptance of self as they understood it, and, more importantly, you have also chosen to live their gains.

Your life program keeps on creating itself through each of your thoughts building upon the other, and the transformation continues until you have taken your last breath. That energy force field grows in strength and opens you up into your Higher—or heavenly—Self. That Higher Self follows you through every thought you think, always encouraging you to create and expand your thinking.

The same goes for the evolution of the human brain. As your intelligence evolves, so, too, does your thinking expand—where your belief in self is your light, and your light becomes your strength; where your strength releases and becomes your success. This is the creation of the Etheric Web.

When we die, our Etheric Web must search for same mind, and personality must attract personality in order to allow this to happen. We are made up of thousands of thoughts, and the thoughts which are the strongest are our astral energies searching for a compatible resonance of their own truth to abide with. Let us take away this fear that you are just one little icon—you are not just one; you are many.

Your Notes:

CHAPTER THIRTEEN

Suicide

Let us now move to another subject in regard to a growing concern that seems to be a tortuous moment in people's lives: suicide. People commit suicide through being caught up emotionally as to a condition that has gone beyond their intellectual control; it is where they have become entangled in their fears of the moment.

They could see no way out, so the ego used all of its control, which collected through the debasement of self and strengthened within them. Suicide can only reach its antenna through the creation of left-brain thinking; its major importance is through the fear of justifying the self. The difference between suicide and natural death is that, when people commit suicide, it is before their natural time of passing (life program).

I have had many interesting contacts who have spoken to me, through the afterlife, about the thoughts they had before they released their attitude of the moment. Notice how I am interpreting this story. They drove themselves to commit suicide through their anger collecting and creating itself through the consequences of not being able to reach beyond the boundaries of their mind. They felt hemmed in! They became trapped through the thought of the moment repeating itself over and over again in their mind. This thought took control and blotted everything else out! In other words, they could not bring a tone or table of justice, into their own behaviour. They could see no other way out; their ego, through its own self-rule, had demanded a judgement.

Their deepest regret is the pain that they allowed others to feel on behalf of what they remember as their last and most important moment. They wish that they could rebalance and release these pent-up thoughts still trapped in their unitedness. All the while, I would explain to them that they still had the opportunity to realign those last moments in order to equate with the law of their own personal thoughts.

More importantly, I would ask them to rethink their last moments, where they realize how their Soul could release to find the freedom of opening them up into their emotional levels, which, in turn, would open up the doorway into the unconscious/higher mind.

Do you see how we must complete our journey into the next realm? I then went on to explain to them the sanctification that they could bring through to their families, from the place where the transformation of their light is living now. So, when someone you know has committed suicide, please explain this paragraph to them through your open heart, and they will be guided into their rightful home. By now, they will know that your thoughts really work!

Please remember the Soul is well above the body before the body stops breathing, so death is painless. It waits for the ego. Someone always comes to help us before we cross to the other side—always remember, we are never left to make the journey alone. We are lovingly guided to our next educational world.

Your Notes:

CHAPTER FOURTEEN

Near-Death Experiences, Visions, And Out-Of-Body Experiences

I would like to explain my education into understanding near-death experiences, as well as the reason why many people slip into their own psyche, mostly due to an accident or shock.

A near-death experience (NDE) is you reaching up into your unconscious/higher mind and searching for a reprieve to support the current level of your own intellect (i.e., in the moment). If you cannot find satisfaction on an inner level, the energy keeps on collecting at every moment, one moment on top of the next, until it becomes an aroused state of mind, where you have hopped up to reach the apex of your antenna. Another name we have used to refer to this experience is a state of "astral travelling", where you wake up as you slip or slide through the boundaries into your unconscious/higher mind. I refer to this area of your mind as a "resting place", where you are being given a second chance at correcting just where your thoughts, through your innocence, have been taken along for the ride.

Once you understand how the Divine Unity of Self collects and communicates back to you, you are able to release extra strands of inner strength, which creates a new sense of freedom for you to go on with the next cycle of life in its entirety. All of this clears your passages of communication, and you can freely come back into your body, in order to extol your thoughts through your own virtues so that you can be delivered up into your next step of intellect.

This experience usually happens to those of you who have overworked your emotions, where your higher mind has delivered you up into the "conduitive arena" of your intellect, and you are on the way to preparing to give yourself a heart attack. Remember that this vicious killer manifests through you squeezing all the joy out of your life. Many stroke victims are also brought into this energy just before the onset of the seizure, which is created through your stubborn rejection of self. There is no need for you to desire to make a victim of yourself. Retrain your thinking; it is much easier on your mind and your body!

You will find similarities throughout my books regarding how the unconscious/higher mind delivers your thoughts back to you. The reason for my repetitive constant reminder is that you have 144,000 personalities (aspects of self), all of which think that they each have their right to claim their fame! Yes, they do when you have organized them in their alphabetical resonance to become your own "new world order"; another way of reminding yourself of this statement is to say that this is the "new order of your world."

If your ego is overriding your thoughts, the amount of pain that the body releases can become excruciating. You have earned your just rewards. Those thoughts have accrued through their mathematics (energy) adding up and reaching the deportment of their own zenith. If you don't move forward through this venture of thought that you have been preparing yourself for, first, you will be warned—and then, if, again, you have not adjusted and reinvested in your thinking, you must pay the price.

When you have an accident and are brought to the hospital in an unconscious state of mind, your conscious and subconscious minds are in abeyance to your unconscious table of atonement. In other words, you have entered up into your "royal throne room". The silence therein is waiting for you, through your ego—or left brain—being brought to rest. You are finally submitting your ego before your emotions, whose home is the right hemisphere of your brain, and, when both hemispheres have harmonized and equalized with one another, the telepathic inheritance of the unconsciousness/higher mind has the right to rule. Therefore, your whole body has succumbed to the deliverance of your inner God/Higher Self within—or brought before your Individual Universal Law of Self and, thereby, the Laws of the Universe. You are being introduced up into a higher kingdom of self, which is what we refer to as the Divine Energy.

It is the Divine Energy that creates and releases your etheric light, which is where you come to an ultimate climax through the thoughts of the Collective Mind/Collective Consciousness—and all that is working beyond your control. I explain it to my business students when I teach them how to open up into their levels of reverence, where they are walking towards their own room of success.

The positive vibrations of your thoughts have multiplied and collected up into these higher realms in order to expand the possibilities of what is happening around you. You can become surrounded by that light—which has collected by itself, and which is emitted back to you through the unconscious/higher mind—and all feels at peace with your world. All of which is the beginning of your first state of euphoria, where the mathematics takes over to escort you into the realms of physics, and that is where your language changes in concordance to your Metaphysics.

Floating above the operating table—out of body experience

Many of you have a vision where you are floating above your bed or the operating table, and you are right that this does happen. Why? You are viewing everything through your third eye (or inner eye), which is available to all through the sight of the unconscious/higher mind. Welcome to my world! You can look down and see what is happening around you, yet you cannot interfere with this wonderful experience until you have physically connected back into your logic thinking, which is connected to your body—and this is what your left brain is all about. You are scientifically looking through yourself, through the "macroscope", where you see through the eternal layers of the Cosmos; not through the microscope, where you are still looking at!

Most of us are immediately filled with fear at this point, and the ego, through allowing that fear to reign supreme, forces us back into the body. I know all about that; I, too, was afraid when I had this experience. In addition to the astral travelling I already mentioned, we sometimes also refer to this as an "out of body experience". It is a natural introduction into the Spiritual essence of the unconscious/higher mind. If you have had that experience once, you certainly can again. You are being offered the opportunity to enter up into the higher realms or worlds of Shamanism.

I explained this information to a group of Egyptologists in Luxor, as I was introducing them to my education regarding the codes of the hieroglyphs. One of them responded, "Oh! You have been privileged to have been allowed to enter into the secret chambers in the Valley of the Kings." No! Not quite right. Over the years of Metaphysical training, I had earned my own footsteps to be welcomed into the Valley of the Kings, as both energies had earned a compatible resonance to become as one.

One of the most life-threatening events is when you are given your life's experiences all over again. You see your life, from your childhood through your teenage years and into adulthood, right up to the given moment. Some of you receive this information in double quick time; others receive it through delayed instalments. It all depends on how you perceive what the story is explaining to you. The entitlement that you allow yourself to receive depends totally on how easily you can release your truth in self.

Now let us take a look at the energy of the visions that you receive from these amazing events. Some of you experience what you see as a horrible nightmare of ghoulish beings, all of which you sense are out to get you.

Wrong! Those beings represent your own personalities (aspects of self) that are still trying to hang on to yesterday's thinking; they try to pull you back by wanting to regain control of your fear. They do not want to take responsibility for themselves, and the Higher Self is reporting back to you where your discrepancies lie.

The religious visions are the ones that we try and hold on to, as our ego feels exempt of all restrictions and is satisfied with the given moment. The futuristic visions are the examples of opportunities that we are able to inherit if we keep on with advancing our thoughts.

A near-death experience is you being allotted a space in your own psyche, where you have the possibility to arch your mind to review in which direction you are heading. Something catastrophic has happened in your life, and you need to be brought back to revisit the direction where you are trying to lead yourself.

Every human has the same experience; it does not matter what language you speak or what age you are. There is only one Collective Consciousness, which is shown to us through many layers of our mind, or the levels of our life experiences.

For instance, a child between the ages of seven and nine years carries the responsibility of the emotional mind of the parent, who is still too afraid to invest and accept his/her own higher intelligence. From the age of nine to eighteen years, the child has accepted the parent's mistakes, and could still be innocently repeating the parent's thinking, to the detriment of child's own future.

Remember, there is only one story, and it is refrained to your ego through the tribal/family law that your Soul has inherited. Our tribal law is the attitude the ego holds onto when it feels insecure with its own behaviour. It has been brought to our attention through the worlds of our emotions—as to how we think, what we feel, and what we hear. We have the right to bring through our first priority; it is where we desire to bring ourselves into satisfying the given moment. Now do you more clearly understand the previous pages? The light that you see in your vision is a co-creation of you through your Individual Universal Law of Self and, thereby, the Laws of the Universe. No difference exists among these experiences; we all receive the same visions. It is through these near-death experiences that you touch and enter into your heavenly home; so, of course, the experience changes your life.

The Shamanic realms await humanity's earnings. Up in these realms there are no wars, and illness is an inheritance of the past. There is a serenity of all things, and, as you ask, so shall you receive. We are all sparks of the one flame. You have earned these rights on your pathway to being delivered up into your Godhead.

CHAPTER FIFTEEN

A Metaphysical Interpretation Of The Egyptian Afterlife And The Interpretation Of The Three Gods "EL", "AN", and "EA", Through Mythology

Over time, many people have taken an interest in searching for the tombs of the Pharaohs; as a result, many countries contributed financially to this endeavour, sending the right people who could offer their educated assistance on such excursions. None of them failed; they all applied their intuition and brought forth a reminder of the hidden language—or the Universal language—that the Egyptians had left us.

In 1922, the responsibility fell on the shoulders of Howard Carter, whose sponsor, Lord Carnarvon of England, released a tremendous amount of money in support of this endeavour; they were just about to abort the digs when a tomb was unearthed. Not just any tomb—Carter unearthed the tomb of Tutankhamen. When the world learned of their find, it created a "Tut" mania.

We note that King Tutankhamen's sarcophagus was created in three stages; the first two were made of wood and rolled in gold leaf, and the third was made of solid gold. Also, the design of the sarcophagus is created in the unconscious/higher recognition of the Asian language, as St John the Divine was explaining to us in the Book of Revelations. We must release the first God "EL" (Everlasting Life) in order to allow the second God "AN" (Ascending through Nourishing) to further educate us into releasing the relationship of self—that is, into becoming the third God "EA" (Energizing the Ascension), as explained to us through the myths.

The rich treasures were brought to the surface, catalogued, and transported to museums, where they were documented even further. Each item in those tombs was a code of emotions designed to carry the young mind of the Pharaoh through to the next step of his journey—or, as we have been taught to call it, to the "afterlife". The findings that fascinated me the most were the "Shabti" that were found in the tomb; these included the figurines that represented one personality (aspect of self) for each day of the year, as well as a group of thirty-six figures that represented each of the twelve strands of the DNA in triplicate—one set for each of the three layers of the Metaphysical Gods ("EL", "AN", and "EA"). I believe that the whole tomb is the combined wisdom of our own personal toolbox, which we keep with us as we journey through the discovery of our self!

We do not have to die physically to reach the afterlife. All it means is that we have reached a zenith of one stage of our intellectual life, and, thus, have earned the choice—or been given the chance—to evolve up to the next advanced stage of our Spiritual life. Remember, your Spiritual life is how you think to do! We can now accept how the myths and biblical stories evolved, passed down from generation to generation, through the language of the Elders who wrote them. Those Elders were the Sages, Prophets, and Scribes. We each are given our own personal riddle at birth, and our journey is to evolve our intellect up into the spheres of telepathic communication; throughout our life, when the ego is in its own repose while we sleep; our dreams begin to inform us through this hidden language. The afterlife, when understood correctly, is the opportunity where we all release ourselves up and into the next phase of humanity's earnings. I bid you welcome to the secret codes that expose the language of Metaphysics. The Gift we were left to go on with is known to us as the Ark of the Covenant. As we release our intellect, we automatically ark ourselves up through those three Metaphysical Gods to become our own Ark. The knower of ways! It has been securely closeted within us forever, and the only way you will find it is through you discovering you. You own it! You are it! It is your brain that returns your thoughts back to you, through your central nervous system, and it will continue to communicate with you through the language of the unconscious/higher mind.

After the tomb was unearthed and catalogued, we know that a mosquito bit Lord Carnarvon on the upper right cheek, and he died soon after. He had earned the mathematics of his thoughts, and his mind had accrued through his own ploy. In other words, through the Divine equation that his Oracle released to him—which was his penance as to how he had to receive his karmic reward—and also through his own innocence, his death was pronounced. Through the importance of this find in Egypt, he had to receive his highest reward, and that was his penance for being jealous of the importance given to Howard Carter for the job that he had accomplished.

Carter returned to London, satisfied with his work. Though it was the biggest archaeological find of his time, Howard Carter died never having received an honour from the British Government for the countless hours of sacrifice that he had committed himself to the discovery of the greatest Seal of Humanity.

I will, I salute the gift he gave us.

"EL", "AN", and "EA" Metaphysically Interpreted from the Myths

In the beginning, there is the story of the God "EL" (Everlasting Life), which represents the home of our ego in relationship to our sexual encounters. These encounters are our basic structure of searching for a placement of our own responsibilities, and, when someone bows before us and does our bidding, we acquaint our earnings through the word control. This is the first doorway to where we connect to our lungs of consciousness, which is where we understand the breath of our inner worlds.

Our next evolution is into the God "AN" (Accepting and Nourishing), where we have understood our primordial earlier worlds through collecting our intelligence and accepting the possibilities of harvesting the seeds we have already sown (our thoughts and deeds). You have entered up into your education system, which is your inner university. Automatically, this subconscious awakening brings the information up to your heart, which opens you up into a belief that you can accomplish anything your mind desires. This is where we shape our characters, and these characters become our personalities, which work with each other to become our support team. They are known throughout the myth as the "lesser Gods".

The combination of this energy then traverses up to connect us into the highest form of intelligence—our unconsciousness/higher mind—that is, to the Divinity of the God "EA", which, through the earlier language, was pronounced "He-ia" (Heavenly Energy of Intelligence Ascending). This is the last of the three prime Gods that we connect to, and it is the home of our heavenly kingdom, which is situated around the crown of the head. It is where we realize that God has a purpose for each and every one of us, and that we have the ability to reconnect back into the origin of our Soul. His purpose is for us to be ensconced into the next generation of our own intuition, which ignites the light within us while we search for and release—or realize—the freedom within. These thoughts are then released down to the next generation for them to abide by. Now we can look back into ourselves and understand more fully the mythical stories that have been handed down through our generations, in order for us to accept that the myth is the question—and that death is the answer.

Your Notes:

CHAPTER SIXTEEN

Past Lives and Reincarnation—A Message From Your Soul

Let's talk about past lives. Through the training from my teachers, I had to learn to focus my mind on my thoughts and live permanently in the moment; I was not allowed to wander in my mind. It was extremely difficult, at first, for me to learn how to control my own energy into how I attracted the next thought.

For me, it began as a game, where I had to learn to focus on one word at a time; as a result, my headaches began to create themselves, and this occurred through me learning to overstep my left brain—or my ego. Sceptics call this imagination! I refer to it as the "image inside my nation".

I was watching how my ego had free rein over my thinking when I was not focusing on myself. This strict education was teaching me how I was sacrificing myself to others. For more than twenty years, I had been a busy mother rearing my children, so most of my thinking was involved in seeing that they were well cared for. I had meals to prepare, clothing to wash, iron, and put away, and housework to keep up with. And I also had all the farm chores to do—the milking, which included making butter and cheese, the gardening, the growing and tending of the vegetables and herbs and flowers—and on and on it went. So, as you can see, for many years my, mind was definitely not focused on myself.

It was as though I was studying six subjects at the same time, and I had to learn how to stretch my time so that my commitment was spread out evenly amongst them all. I had never been one to attract headaches, so, when they began to occur, I wondered what they were all about. I realized that they were busily creating themselves through me overriding the plan that my ego was trying to submit to me. Slowly, I learned to slow down my brain waves until I was in control of every thought released from my mind.

In reference to a vision of a "past life experience", each time you receive through your vision world, it is a visual interpretation of an interruption that is going on in your mind in the present moment. You are holding onto some thought which is able to retard your ability to move up to the next stage of your intellectual growth. The eternal energy of your Soul is giving this to you in a metaphor, and you immediately turn your back on this story through your innocence of not understanding what the inner experience is trying to explain to you; as a result, you have difficulty accepting the consequences that go along with it.

Let us say that you visit a consultant/therapist who is about to explain to you what they are receiving in their vision world. This person says to you, in his/her innocence, "I see that you were a man who was beheaded in a past life." The metaphor of the vision represents something that you are doing, in that moment, to one of your 144,000 personalities (the 12x12, aspects of self). The correct interpretation is explaining to you that you are strangling your own power. How did the therapist receive this vision? Through the language of the unconscious/higher mind, because there is only one story, and it is released back to us, metaphorically, in a parable, just like the hieroglyphs on the walls in Egypt—and it is up to us to work it out! This world is an exact replica of the same world we enter when we die! Once we have learned to silence the mind, we can all tune into this hidden language.

A "lifetime" (Metaphysically interpreted) is the experience of a thought in the moment, and a "reincarnation" is you collecting your thoughts to begin a new experience. In other words, you are beginning to reinvest in yourself again. For example, I am a facet of my father, and so are my children and grandchildren and now my great grandchildren. I look at my grandsons, and I see the same walk and stance of my father reflecting through them. This is how we inherit the hidden language we autonomically collect through the DNA.

If we learn to accept the original story, we will free our fears, and the next moment could appear to change the shape of our destiny. We are dying and rebirthing all the time; we birth our next thought by dying to our previous thought. As our intellect releases from the bondage that the family placed around it, we can understand how our language changes, and how the thought that we have just let go of becomes a past life, and then, through each new thought, we reincarnate in the moment.

In the beginning of my transference into the education of the Shamanic principles, many people came and asked me for a past-life reading. I would ask them why this was so important to them. "I want to know who I was in a past life," was the cry of some. I would tell them that they were the release of their parents' thoughts. They would say, "But, what about my previous existence? I am having these terrible dreams; I think I have to revisit this past life to bring myself to task. Let me tell you about last night's dream." So, as I listened to their innocence explaining itself, I would begin to create a Metaphysical story to satisfy the curiosity of their inner child in order to explain their dreams back to them. That "previous existence" is the thought they have in this moment—there is nothing "past" about it; it is an experience that needs an adjustment in the right here and right now.

We continue on now to explain another short story regarding reincarnation. Every church has been placed on what is referred to as "pagan land"—or, through the Metaphysical language, the "pages of 'AN'". We know by now, through myth, that we earn the home of the second level through reaching our temperance—that is, walking up, into, and with the God "AN". This level reminds us of who we can become, which can only occur through us understanding the education of our inner self. These stories have been passed down to us for thousands of years, in every culture, long before Christianity rewrote these same stories, which were gathered through the understanding of the myths and through the interpretations of the principles of Egypt and Greece.

That "pagan land" is a force field of electromagnetic energy, which humans have created and supplied through opening up their hearts to complement their own belief as to how they learned to understand their feelings and accept themselves. These force fields are spheres of light that have gathered and have been ritualized through human acknowledgement of self-worth—all of which created the ceremony within. The churches realized all this, and so they needed to take over that energy as well. The word "Church", as my father explained it to me, is a "gathering of ideas". Through the codes, the word "ch-ur-ch", interprets as, "the energy of our DNA releasing itself up through our spinal column"; and this we know is protected by our vertebrae. This energy releases through us understanding the relationship between our self and the light of God that is reflected throughout every cell of our body; it is what we call our "Divinity". Therefore, our Divinity is "our way of life"; it becomes a principal witness of self.

I would like you to understand that, metaphysically, we begin again every time we release—that is, any time we die to any moment; in this way, we are learning to unravel the DNA that we have inherited. Our past history then has the opportunity to listen to our next positive active thought, which, through our ultra consciousness, automatically transforms our DNA. Death—and dying—is the transformation of self.

All this is in relationship to how our lymphatic system functions. The lymphatic system is extremely important in its function as a heavenly outpost, watching and securing us as we earn the acceptance of mastering our self.

Our lymph regenerates itself through us returning—or nurturing—our energetic thoughts back through our body. I teach my students that this most important system is, metaphorically speaking, the "umbrella of God". This system is permanently returning us back to the challenges that we are applying to our self. In this case, if we are yearning to keep harmonizing our mind, we challenge our personalities (aspects of self) to do likewise; and, by accepting this challenge, we are permanently moving forward. Again, this is another explanation of the conquest for achieving everlasting life—or, to accepting the consequences of what we refer to as our "past lives".

If we can accept this informative advice, it will allow the inner library (our DNA), which is the make-up of the Soul, to astutely redesign the thoughts for our next generation. Our mathematics then has the opportunity to rearrange the next generation's quest of intellect. The transition always continues. It is like stocktaking in the business sector, where we must add what is left over from the last year's trading against our assets in order to recognize how the business is functioning. Through this confirmation, the next challenge places itself on our horizon. This then sets an example as to how confidently we can continue earning our rewards.

The unconscious/higher mind lives in the world of symbolism; this is where our thoughts refract on an inner level, becoming a symbolic structure through the mathematics of the Collective Consciousness. This is the world of truth—or the "Ma'at-he-Ma'at-ic's" of the mind—and it creates the worlds of the invisible, which we can only see through the exemplification of our belief in self. Symbolism is created through the geometry that equates through the mathematics of the mind; and, this can only occur when we have balanced each hemisphere of the brain, which autonomically opens up through being measured by our belief. This is also where we have earned the right to enter up into the Divinity of the unconscious/higher mind.

Symbolism is the only language that our brain absorbs in order to create the function of the next moment. We still sleep, work, and live our everyday existence. It is the world of our co-creation, which allows each thought to collect up into its zenith, and, once that peak has accomplished its own design, it releases its hold over us in order for us to begin again.

Your journey of life is all about you unravelling your Individual Universal Law of Self and understanding those laws that were heralded down to you. We cannot remain the same, and, if we do not move forward, we become stagnant. Through lack of development, we are open to attracting dis-ease. When you believe and trust in yourself, your mind becomes balanced, and then you come to the level of emotional intelligence where you realize that your laws work for you.

CHAPTER SEVENTEEN

A Principal Law of Shamanism

I would like to explain an important principal law of Shamanism. The Law of the Universe—this "Hidden God"—states that, as you earn the right to evolve up into the High Priest or Shaman in order to become the Prophet, you must go through the process of metaphysically dying three times; this is a natural surge to connect up into the Ascension Process. More is eloquently explained in my book "Decoding the Shaman Within".

Many of you have come to me and said, "I think I died last night. I felt my body split into fragments like a giant jigsaw puzzle, and I had to rearrange each piece and place all these fragments back together again." Through the Shamanic philosophies, we refer to this as "rearranging the original mosaic of the DNA".

Some of you have left over pieces from your past inherited thinking, and yet you feel you have completed your picture, which by now looks slightly different from the original one you had. You have difficulty seeing where these pieces were originally connected. That is a good sign; it shows you where you have re-sorted your mind and died to scenes of your past, which are now no longer applicable for you to hold on to for support. This code, when interpreted, alerts us to the fact that we are being reminded of the three Metaphysical Gods ("EL", "AN", and "EA") evolving into the one God/Higher Self. It is explaining the codes of how the mathematics (energy) began to collect through the three different dimensions of our mind.

Through these three exemplified deaths, your journey informs you that your ego has to deplete in order for your fear to subside through your own discernment. On three different occasions, these codes state that you must finish your old life completely and begin to rebuild a new you. This first inherited death completes itself at the moment when you have nearly finished earning the second God "AN", which is educating the self up into accomplishing the throne of adulthood. The final initiation collects when you have entered up into the unconscious/higher mind of humanity's awareness. I had to learn to construct and build my bridge through bringing the codes together to equate and balance the next thought that came to me, rather than trying to push myself towards it. By this time, I realized how I could slide into all those parallel worlds of continuing dimensions in order to be in heaven and on the earth at the same time.

The first time this happened in my life I just went with the flow; there was no way I could stop or interfere with its process. I knew that I had to go through a rebirthing technique which spoke to me in a coded language that was far beyond my logical control. My next world could then open up the next step of my intelligence, where my energy became lighter. It was as though I knew all the answers before they were asked. As my brain accepted and accrued with my reality, I could understand how the Collective Consciousness worked through the power of death releasing itself; it was an ethereal feeling of self-worth. As each stage presented itself to me, I became more aware of how this process worked.

The lessons are the same for those who have just died and passed over. This knowledge allowed me to help many to adjust to their new frequencies as they entered into the next world.

Your teacher or this Hidden God within asks you to move on, and that means that you must close every door to your past inheritance and leave it behind. You are given the privilege of accepting the responsibility of self; whether you are right or wrong depends on your level of self-love and intellect. Your Soul energy becomes your intelligence, which, in turn, becomes the essence of your intelligence, and we know that is your Spirit—or your "spirit-duality" where the two hemispheres of your brain co-join with one another to become one.

All the dreams that never came to their own fruition will now be freely available to you. They never went anywhere, and they will belong to you—they are your manifestation. Mine waited for me until I earned the responsibility to symbolically die to my previous existence.

For twenty years, I had the same vision: I wanted a big kitchen with lots of cupboard space and big benches, where I could lay out twenty plates and serve a meal to everyone at the same time. I wanted a window in the roof so that I could open up the room on hot days and send the energy out to the heavens. I wanted cupboards that were huge drawers, so that I did not have to bend down to search for what I wanted. After I had finally completed my journey, a house became available in the area where I was asked to work in—this was not just a house, this was the house, complete with the kitchen of my dreams. Unfortunately, by that time, I was the only person I had to serve meals to. You see, I had finally earned and been given exactly what I asked for!

Slowly, other dreams released themselves for me, where I was invited to Europe to lecture in two Universities in Europe. I lived in a large château (castle), with fifty-five beautiful rooms, situated on eight acres of magnificent parklands, including trees that reached for the heavens. I was still on my own, but I knew that I had earned every measure of my lifestyle—I had become my dream.

Your Notes:

CHAPTER EIGHTEEN

Allow the Old Thoughts To Die To Your Past, The Moment Of Death And Grieving

Allow me to explain to you as you evolve through this life, that it is very important for you to allow the old thoughts to place themselves into your memory bank, where they do not hinder or become a burden to your past. The Gospel of Phillip contains a wonderful story in regards to this previous sentence. Jean-Yves Leloup translated and interpreted this story from the Coptic original, and he explains that the story that was written on the 111th plate: "The Teacher went into Levi's dye works; he took seventy-two colours and threw them into the vat, and when he took them out, they were all white: He said, "This is how the son of man has come, like a Dyer."

These seventy-two colours are also the number of the Sacred Names of God throughout the ancient laws, through the equation $8 \times 9 = 72$. The number eight (8) represents "balance and harmony through the infinite"—or infinity. This is multiplied by the number nine (9), which represents the "knowing of self". Mathematically, they add up to seventy-two (72).

The number seven (7) represents the "inner teacher", connecting to the number two (2), which represents the "relationship to self". In other words, the inner teacher is the relationship of knowing our self. Once the rainbow connects through the final "arcing of the covenant", all the colours blend as one. Do not keep the old alive; it automatically becomes a member of your Divine Inheritance. We have named the past a "memorial cenotaph of the mind"—please, always take your next positive step forward.

When the energy (Soul) leaves the body, that body begins its deterioration process. The energy of the light force of the planet overtakes the body, and it returns to the earth. If the body is cremated, the energy of the fire consumes the body, which becomes ash; thus, the body, in turn, becomes the fire. The fire is the resurrection. If everyone understood those beautiful words, "Ashes to ashes, and dust to dust", no one would need to grieve. Grieving is only created through guilt, guilt is created through fear, and fear is the creation of the ego. When it comes time for our next step, we realize that our ego is the child, and the child represents the word "innocence". Goodness, it pays to reverse everything you think! Doesn't it? Now we can make it easier on ourself, and all learn to bring our lives up into an eternal balance.

On an unconscious level, the person who died unconsciously has accepted their own program, including their moment of passing through into their next dimension, which is also embedded into the mathematics of the planet. This is the procreation (professional creation) of consciousness. Not many people know the moment of death until their time comes, and yet, there is never a mistake. What is this wonder that we all live amongst? Death is created through the mathematical thoughts earning the right for that person to come into their own fruition (fruitfulness, accomplishment, success) of the Collective Consciousness—whether we are thinking about the self or on behalf of the planet as a whole.

When I counsel those who are grieving, I suggest that they go back and understand the conversations that they had with the deceased in their last few days. It is just amazing what we can remember. Those conversations, which could have been spoken or telepathically shared, represent the Metaphysical language releasing itself. The unconscious/higher mind prepares all parties concerned for the appropriate liaison that allows for the release. Even in the event of an accidental death, if you go back over the most recent conversations—especially your thoughts three days prior to the death—you will notice how the Collective Consciousness was preparing you for this major event.

As you evolve to open up your third eye; you will see the Souls who have passed over, as there is nowhere for them to go! They are all still here. Why? Once we enter up into this higher vibration we are able to read the Collective of all, and these are the thoughts of the planet echoing back to us our freedom through the "Divine Inner Relationship" that we all have with one another. The more advanced you become to bringing yourself up into the unconscious/higher mind, the more solidified that Soul appears to be. Each level explains a different discernment. Whilst we have a fear of death, we also hold onto our support garments (thoughts) through holding onto the fear of understanding our self.

I have been inundated with the young ones who have died in multiples through global catastrophes (e.g. the Afghanistan and Iraq War, tsunamis, floods, earthquakes, and other catastrophic awakenings). They are so pleased to be able to speak to those of us here on the earth who have become aware of how to converse with them. They share with us the dreams they had, although they never had the opportunity to experience many of them; they treat us to their royalness, and they also release to us their disappointment in not achieving their vows, their dreams, their thoughts that were not ready to eventuate. When will we ever learn—and, more importantly, when will we ever earn? I thank you for reading this chapter.

Your Notes:

CHAPTER NINETEEN

Questions Regarding Energies and Entities

Here is a series of questions and answers regarding energies. I hope that, through them, you will find the answers to some of your own.

Question: I am a therapist. Are there Souls who hang onto other people's force fields and devour their energies? I have had the experience of an entity being left behind after the patient had left my clinic. I asked the entity to go into the light. Was that the right thing to do?

Answer: As their therapist, you must look at your patients from an astral level—that is, through the unconscious/higher mind. From that level, you may see "beings"—or living energies—that either hook onto or into your patients' bodies to grab hold of them. These are energy forces manifesting themselves through the thinking of those patients. Those energies represent a blocked emotion in those patients, so, when we bring this information back into the present reality, it is just the patients attacking themselves; in other words, it is the force field of those patients re-creating their own existence. It is not an entity from somewhere else.

Do you think that God (Greatest Oracle of the Divine) made a mistake? Consciousness is a mirror of our thinking, and, in the psychic, cognitive world, we can easily become confused when we are in the process of learning to understand how to see the reflections of someone else's thoughts. Some call this "metatron energy", which releases to those who have earned the right to see. The consciousness mutates through corresponding with the energy into a physical form. In your vision world, you saw an energy that was of a consequence to that patient's thinking, and so, when the patient left, you were left with the energy that you saw.

How and why did this energy leave the patient to come and stay with you? The energy will do exactly as you ask—it will go to your light, rather than search for its own, as your light is closer and also brighter. You will feel energies around you all the time; this is an integral part of you discovering your inner education, which will lift you up into these higher kingdoms of intelligence. It is your own Soul light that is attracting the patient to you in the first place! The energies that you see manifest in another person's body are all in relationship to your own fears. They are a chemical compound of consciousness that relate to you, through the levels of your intelligence, and that is why you can see them. You are the Alchemist who is calling those exemplified neurons, which created these thoughts, to spring to your attention.

People manifest those fears through being too afraid; another word I like to explain is their innocence as to how they can begin to learn to understand themselves. An energy force is only that person's thinking, and it is attaching to the body through an etheric level. The entity that was left behind in your clinic is a message for you! What do you need to change regarding your own thoughts? Energy attracts attention. Please remember God did an absolute brilliant job in designing us!

No one who has died can ever come back to haunt us; we do that to ourselves through not listening to the messages of our own judicious wisdom. That goes for haunted houses as well. What we see from this experience is a message for you; it is not a message from the other side. The ego can play magnificent games to keep itself in control of you. God bless you as you begin to understand—and, now, enjoy—the search for the intelligence of this Hidden God.

Question: When I am in a half-sleep state at night, I see entities, and they seem very real to me. Why is that?

Answer: It is the expansion of your own Soul. You are in a waking dream state of mind. Your aura is the vibration that comes from your Soul, and those astral bodies manifest inside your aura. Astral bodies are symbolically formed through your thinking. When we are in that lucid dreaming state of mind, we are bordering between worlds. You are on the edge of allowing your mind to enter into the unconscious/higher mind of the Collective Consciousness. Remember, you own and are responsible for 144,000 personalities (the 12x12, aspects of self, according to our DNA and the last book of the Bible, Revelations, which is the revealing of our inner nations!) which live within that plane of unconscious/higher energy, which are free to manifest throughout the worlds of your thinking. When you feel and see energies moving within, out of, and around your aura—or your Soul energy—once again, these are your own thoughts, through the mind of your ego, that child within, mirroring your story back to you. I am just bringing common sense back into the picture here. Stop fantasizing, you have better things to do with your time!

Your Soul's journey is through the vibrational energy that releases from your thoughts—whether that be positive or negative energy. This is your life force collecting your consciousness in order for you to understand, through your innocence, where you are yearning for information; you also have an inner urge to awaken every cell in your body. They are awake, you know; it is your ego, on a conscious level, that is in the process of accepting your self. The more you awaken on an inner level, the more your energy begins to solidify, which releases itself from the restrictions you have placed around it, and it begins to walk on the outside of you—all of which heightens your intelligence. Your Soul is your "hidden" intelligence until you become aware of it, and, when you understand that, your Soul releases from its bondage to become your Apostolate, and then it continually works with and on behalf of you.

The only entity that is trying to take over your body is your new energy, which becomes your new light. Your ego is not too happy about that new growth, so the dark side of you tries to strengthen itself. Again, these are the worlds of fear that you create through not understanding your Divinity. You are entering into the place where all your fears come together, which the Bible refers to as "Armageddon" (Revelations 16:16).

The Law of the Universe does not allow others to possess us. No one has the right to place his/her distemper onto us, unless we innocently allow it. Usually, that permission is only given through the gift of love—that is, when we sacrifice ourselves to others. You know the old saying "as above, so below". When you are on your life's quest, you learn to accept, through your new responsibility, that all these energies are your own; they are the reflections of your thinking. They are the Karma or "Kha-Rha-Mha" that you innocently give to yourself. Everything has a life force, and everything deals with itself, if it is free to view through its own illusion.

We create our own darkness, again and again, through our rejection of self; we desperately try to put the blame onto somebody else, as we do not want to receive the consequences of what we have done to ourselves. Those suppressed dark worlds are the ones that create the "fantasy", and the light worlds are the ones that create the "fun-to-see". Understand that our fear is with us at all times—until we have earned the freedom in the mind to allow it to release itself. Up to that point, our fear is our driving force, and we cannot live without it. That fear is our ego rebounding back into its own self-acclaim, and, through you accepting your inner equation—or the responsibility that you now understand regarding self—you can see how it manipulates your well-being and how it wants to seize control.

Now can you understand the world of "Depression" that so many of us find so very easy to slip or slide into as a safety harness, in place of releasing our spiritual strength!!!! Or have you put it in a basket and shoved it behind the door to view at a later time or maybe you have swept it under the carpet, where you walk along a bumpy road and trip over yourself time and time again to remind you of what excuses you have released and allowed to control your fear.

Find the strength to love your own insecurities—your fear, which is the child within us all. That child must grow up—or spiral up—into becoming the adult. The word "spiral" refers to the place where we have the opportunity to turn around and accept our self, at the exact moment when the positive energy steps forward to offer itself to us.

Change the word "entity" to "energy"; your energy is your God-ness reflecting your thinking back to you in Cinemascope. Those entities seem to be from another world; entities are logical left-brain thinking, and energies are emotional right-brain thinking. Maybe now you can see how your own ignorance of something you do not understand has created that fear within. Welcome to my world!

Nelson Mandela once said, "We are not afraid of the dark, we are afraid of the light, through not knowing how to use it."

Your Notes:

CHAPTER TWENTY

I Am My Temple

As our aura—or Soul energy—sends impulses back into the body, the brain takes over and releases, in a pictographic language, what many of us refer to as our imagination. I call it the "image inside my nation", which is how I describe my visions from God. I am a child of God, and, through my innocence, I am being reimbursed with a message about something I am not seeing correctly. It is how we understand and interpret the message that seems to get us into trouble. The code for the numbers of 144,000 is "I am my own temple, my temple is my temple, 1-4-4, and I am reflecting back to me the mind—000—of my Soul." It is one side of the brain talking to the other. So, at the moment when we are viewing ourselves correctly, our thinking is the moment that this thought reaches its own zenith and disappears, and then we rebirth into the next one. If we stay disciplined and focused in our own thinking, the world would automatically correct and create its own responsibility. I would love you to think that sentence over, many times as I had to do. Also to do with that word "depression".

The "Quest of Life" is our journey of self-discovery. We are thinking and creating that journey through the acceptance of the connection which is every person's inner Spiritual aim: to move up into the unconscious/higher mind.

The physical body that we have now is only here for this lifetime, so please remember, our energy upon leaving that body will still be here, as that energy is how we were all created since time began. We are the representation of this whole planet. The symbolic number of 374 billion cells that are in our make-up—or is it 6 trillion cells; no, recently I heard that we had around 8 trillion cells, and we are still counting—are all in tune with the rest of the Collective Consciousness, therefore you are not just you, you are also a reflection of every other person on this planet.

A Chinese philosopher once said to me, "Why do you long

noses celebrate a birth, yet mourn a death? You Westerners have it all upside down; you should celebrate the death and mourn the birth." I now understand what he meant, although it took quite a few years of education for me to earn that understanding. The Asian principles are aware, through their understanding of what they have earned thousands of years before our wisdom; that is to say, they have already earned their right to live up in the unconscious/higher mind. We still have to reach up in our intelligence in order for us to be able to echo ourselves to their level.

We have the ability to symbolically live 10 million lives during this earthly life. During my training, I had to play out one thought with my 144,000 personalities or aspects of self. I had to watch as that one thought reached its own zenith, exhausted itself, and disappeared. During the death of that thought's process, the next thought had to follow through on the energy of that one releasing itself. The moment must continue through our mucus for the next thought to reincarnate itself. I could take my time, so I watched as time extended itself to suit my recollections.

Create your own book, beginning with this idea: "the story of me getting to know me". Practice this game and see how long you last. I know I tried many times! It is a fascinating thing to do when the mind is in abeyance to the self.

Reincarnation is the process of birthing of one thought and allowing it to play out its role before you are given the opportunity to birth the next. Be careful that you don't repeat the same lifetime again. Isn't that why you are here? Each one of you have already lived millions of lifetimes, and you are continually doing so, moment by moment.

Stop this childish attitude that is retarding your thinking—it keeps your mind contained! Move over and allow the adult to come through, as the Adult is the next step before the Adept. It is one thought allowing the next thought, allowing the next thought, allowing the next thought, and so on. You have lost no energy; through the freedom of your mind, you have simply allowed. Understand the preciousness of your next thought, as it is embedded with the previous one, and must follow on from this current one. Learn to bring all your lifetimes together in this life, and enjoy!

No matter how hard we try, when we let that thought go, the following thought is always a mirror reflecting its next level to us. This is created around the mastoid area behind the ears.

As you learn to understand yourself, you will accept that this solidifies the belief in self; and, through you believing in self, you begin to trust yourself. Through trusting in self—and listening to your God-ness within—you become everlasting life, right now, living your existence on this planet. Don't wait until you die! Remember, consciousness is registered and created layer by layer. That goes for you too!

We have the opportunity to manifest ourselves again and again. We can live forever, as we are this everlasting life. "Everlasting life" means "your Spiritual action releasing itself"—or, as we now understand it, the introduction into the world of the unconscious/higher mind.

The Universe is never-ending. Just as we begin, so too, do we end: at the beginning. When we come through the wisdom of consciousness, we are a wonderment to our family, and then to ourselves,—as we yearn to learn and earn—the rights to our own passage. We grow and have the opportunity to experience every facet of life while we are here. This eternal energy is everlasting, and it is freely available for you to have at your disposal the moment you ask yourself a question. That is the cycle of life. Death is just a new beginning. It is a repeat performance of what you have lived here; the only difference is that there is no ego to argue with you. You have entered into the right hemisphere of your intelligence, where we find that Love is abounding and unconditional. Understand, accept, and have the ability now to act out in your new found freedom and joy for the rest of your life.

CHAPTER TWENTY ONE

The Afterlife For Adults

I have been asked by many people over the last thirty five years to explain how their departed partner, son, daughter or parents have progressed on the other side. The questions ranged from: "Are they happy or have they met up with the rest of the family?" "Did they get my message and are they aware of the new grandchildren that have birthed since their passing?" The questions were endless.

More to the point, I have become aware of how my information has changed since I first began to deliver a message to someone on the other side and I heard their reply. Was I right in my answers? Did I get their son's or daughter's name right? Was I speaking the truth of what the departed was informing me of? Was that me inventing a story when I was counselling someone who came to see me regarding the departed? I had to bolster my courage and trust that the truth would be revealed.

Over the years that followed, I was truly amazed at how I settled into the discovery of being in two different worlds at the same time. I was there in the afterlife and yet I was sitting in my office right here on earth, talking to the parent or granddaughter who wanted to know what her granny was doing in heaven. Over time and well over 100,000 consultations later, my intelligence expanded and my fear abated, and I could just prattle on. We have all had a jolly good laugh at some of the stories I received, from both sides.

When we pass over, we are guided to where we need to be delivered. If we are elderly and have been ill for quite a while or have had an accident, we are shepherded into Chapel and stay there until we are healed. The angelic realms take over, and their healing commences to calm the departed person down. The patients all so lovingly talk about this place and very often give a running commentary on how majestic and calm this Chapel is. So, have no fear in regards to the damaged minds or bodies of people who are on the other side, as they are taken very good care of by the most devoted light beings who wish to serve. The reason it is called the Chapel, is not only for religious purposes, it is a place of healing the mind as well as the body. Both are appropriate, don't you think! Remember the word religion in Latin, is "religio", meaning "binding oneself to linking back into the Soul". And this is also with the Chapel in the hereafter.

When the departed are fully aware of their surroundings, they then have the opportunity to move around and explore further. I have many reports from them through this endeavour. I have laughed away their hours of explanations and shed my tears, at their fears of the unknown. As they become familiar with the afterlife, their own mind becomes more relaxed as they begin to realize they are in a safe place and all is well. Their family quickly come together for them, where the departed meet up with sisters, brothers and parents who make them feel welcome and bring them up to date, as all members on the other side can fill them in on many stories of events, as they can see everything from up there to down here, much clearer than many of us can from down here. People on the other side spend a tremendous amount of time searching for familiar contacts apart from family members as they become familiar with the afterlife.

If their threads of consciousness of the newly departed are still connected to the family left behind, many of them desperately want to send a message back, that they are okay. This is when we are connected and I can honestly say you will come for a reading and their message will be passed on to you. It is when you walk out of my office with a smile on your face that I know all is given at the right time.

Many of my students have passed over and I had instant contact with them, always with an important message for those of the family, who are left behind and are grieving for them. "I am finally pain free and feel nice and warm", are many of the messages. "I can see and hear or speak, for the first time", are others. "Wow, look at the colours", many say. "I will bring you into contact with someone who can help you", is a big one, and this is where we step into your picture to release, your fear of the unknown.

My own personal friends are back from the other side as quick as they left! And what a transformation. The women are dressed differently in mainly Grecian long flowing pastel robes etc., as they transform back through their life path and become younger and younger. The men seem to choose their favourite clothes that they chose to wear at certain times throughout their life. Some of them are very appropriately dressed as though they are off to a Majestic ball, and look so incredibly handsome. A big message from the men is to tell their wives to please lay the pillows down the length of their body and cuddle the pillows as though they are still with their wives at night for comfort.

The more the departed maturate into their new home on the other side, is when their next education begins; which gives them the opportunity to delve into what is unfinished business down here. Once accomplished, they are then given the opportunity to begin new teachings on how their own mathematics (thinking) has matured to lead them down a different pathway.

New friendships are formed, as well as new temperaments and personalities are created. The most important gift that I can give is for you to realize that they are always able to see all from the other side. They come to you in your hour of need. They are there to want to hug and cuddle you, to kiss your children, their grandchildren good night and rock them to sleep. It is truly amazing how many children are aware of this in their innocence and have the most amazing stories to tell.

Hoping this chapter helps you understand, how the collective of the mathematics of the consciousness (Collective Consciousness) is all connected, where we all have the opportunity to see or hear all in this universe once you have opened your heart to yourself! It is not hard, just love you for being you, and learn to appreciate who you are. Let the other side in and go to sleep, your dreams will send you the pictures of what you need to know. Remember they are only a thought away.

May you inherit this knowledge, through your "God given

Right" to know it is all very positive; there is no negative in heaven that is a fallacy relayed from your own fear. May you be blessed forevermore.

Thank you for reading my explanations on Decoding Death. Love Omni.

Appendix A—Short Summary Format

Death and the Universe:
The Universe is never-ending. Just as we begin, so do we end: at the beginning. When we come through the wisdom of consciousness, we are a wonderment to our family, and then to ourselves. We grow and have the opportunity to experience every facet of life while we are here. This Universal eternal energy is everlasting, and it is freely available for you to have at your disposal the moment you ask yourself a question. That is the cycle of life. Death is just a new beginning. It is a repeat performance of what you have lived here; the only difference is that there is no ego to argue with you. Love is abounding and unconditional.

Death is of Your Design:
Death is of your own design; it is a sacrament that is constantly programming itself between you/and the mathematical attainment of your Higher Self and God/which is the Collective truth of your personal Consciousness. There is a program for every human on this planet, and that program must be adhered to and fulfilled; it must be fulfilled through the codes that represent the mathematics of your Soul.

Where is your soul?:
Your Soul is your life's energy, your energy is your force field, and your force field is your aura, (the aura is the energy that is produced within your cells). Your Soul is the energy that collects from your unconscious/higher mind. Your unconscious mind is the gathering of your forefathers and foremothers minds; this is the life force of your DNA. Please remember that it is through the last strand of our DNA that we have continued to remain emotionally aware on this planet; it is that twelfth strand that we call "love", which has the collective presence to support and hold all the other strands together.

Your Soul's journey is through the vibrational energy that releases from your thoughts—whether that is positive or negative energy. This is your life force collecting your consciousness in order for you to understand, through your innocence, where you are yearning for information; you also

have an inner urge to awaken every cell in your body.
Your Soul is your "hidden" intelligence until you become aware of it, and, when you understand that, your Soul releases from its bondage to become your Apostolate (a leader of reform), and then it works with and on behalf of you.

On your life's journey, you will die to, and grow away, from your old ways of thinking. Through your own assertion, you will learn to release your fear through finding enough courage, strength, and power to believe that you are a miracle (a "mirror of your cell").

What and how you are thinking right now is the result of what you have become; what you are doing on this journey of life is also learning to understand where you have come from. The abilities and opportunities you have understood so far will determine where you can go on to complete your journey of self-discovery. While you are living this journey you are also in a process of dying, and, from death, a new life begins—it is a continuous cycle. No matter what thought you have in your mind, your energy travels around inside your aura and must always reconnect back to the beginning of its source, before you have completed the thought. This then allows the thought to release back into the Collective Consciousness through the complement of yourself. When your intellect or your unconscious/higher mind is ready to separate from your body, death becomes imminent.

It can take days, weeks, or years before your matrix collects and is measured through equalizing your mathematics back into its original source. The outcome of this—whether simple or complex—will all depend on your own intellectual belief. Why the difference in time for this process? Some people retain a semiconscious connection with the body, through the remaining threads of ego or fear, once the Soul begins to release. Our fear, which we have inherited and systematically created, is hanging on through our lack of trust or belief in self. Fear will continue to remain caught up in the body, until we can feel the freedom of our thoughts associated with this word trust, and then, when we come to the point of acceptance, the fear will appear to disentangle and release itself. This occurs through you revisiting the experiences of your life's moments, after which time, the Soul is free to go on to its next journey.

<u>The Quantum Hologram and when we die</u>:
As we are about to die, the Soul expands its belief and slowly releases up autonomically into the next parallel world. We refer to the afterlife by many names: "dimensional time-shifting", "cellular recognition", "holographic imprints", and "parallel worlds". The Soul learns to disentangle the strands that the ego—or fear—had wrapped around it, for support, throughout the physical body. Those energies then change and grow through the gift that you are adhering to them. Your energy can never die; your antimatter can leave your matter. That antimatter is what we call "etheric energy"—or the electromagnetic energetic light waves—that vibrate and coerce with one another right throughout the Soul energy of the planet.

The Quantum Hologram that is the creation of all of us is comprised of these electromagnetic waves that cohere until they become coherent, and then they reform themselves. The higher and more powerful your vibrations become through accepting your intelligence and wisdom, the more your waves have the opportunity to become aware of their capability of separating—through which you will have the strength to regenerate the self. String theories are at work here.

Those threads of energy multiply and become your power force, where it transforms into your Etheric Web—that is, the web of your Divine Consciousness, which is spread permanently out there, repeating itself throughout the Collective Consciousness, forevermore. Through the principles of Shamanism, we have named this experience "unconditional love". After death, these layers of love filter back down through your family.

Our Soul begins to gather and collect its web, and it departs from the body days before our death—or when the mind accrues into its own stabilization, in order to allow the body to slow down. Some Souls begin to bounce outside their body up to eight weeks or more before they die, although the program of their existence must be initiated and mathematically completed before they are allowed to leave the planet.

What are the three stages of death from disease?:
There are three stages of death for us to understand; I will explain them to you through my interpretation.

The number one (1) in Sacred Numerology represents "I am"

This information equates through the conscious mind of self, which is the responsibility of the egotistical left brain, and, when it is in doubt, it turns to register its thoughts through to the subconscious mind—that is, the emotional right brain. Of course, it expects to pass on the responsibility of what it has created to someone else. This gives it freedom in the moment, and it thinks it can continue on in its merry way. That is why the ego has no continuation in its memory banks. It has difficulty holding onto a momentous thought, and the only way it can nourish itself is through relying on what has already been!

Your emotional mind collects these vibrations and converts them into feelings, which are flushed throughout your system, where they are automatically collected and brought up through to your pituitary gland—this is the doorway into the Divine energy, which is your unconscious mind (Soul). This mind becomes aware of your inner stutter, where your ego is beginning to lose its self-control. Your higher mind holds the energy of every cell in your body, and it hears your ego placing your thinking into the "too hard basket", uttering, "But what about me? I AM!" By using the word "but" in the beginning of your sentence, you have already begun to create your next excuse! The unconscious mind begins to coerce with the ego; and this is where your other senses begin to understand what it has created for itself.

Stage One of Death is for your ego to learn who you are, and then accept that you are about to head towards an end of the old experiences that it has contained for itself! The body is doing what comes naturally, and so this is where you have the opportunity to learn how to surrender to yourself. Time which is created through the fourth dimension; will become the ego's teacher. The liver begins to empty out its aggression, and it voluntarily tips the residue into the gall bladder for it to be converted. When you are living out the thought processes of how you have lived your life—and when you are in doubt in regards to it—you automatically pass yourself onto the next coherent moment.

<u>The number two (2) in Sacred Numerology represents "the relationship to self"</u>

When you reach your state of acceptance, Stage Two of Death begins to step forward into your psyche. In some people, this second stage can be a very bitter part of the game of death; it is a time when the channels of your thoughts open to remembering and releasing your past experiences back to you. It does not begin with the happier times. The ego will have a tendency to remind you of the bitterness that occurred throughout its life—when it could not get its own way—and it will automatically look for the shortcomings of all the experiences that were regaled upon you. It must learn to come back into the relationship of self.

This area is what we call the "gall energy", and the gall bladder is the organ—or "planet"—in your own "Universe", where you store your toxic chemicals. As previously mentioned, this organ has the responsibility to filter the anger from your liver and collect the bitterness of the suspended fear that you have already created. The gall bladder now comes into its own realization: that it must cleanse this anger and purge itself before death. The memories that it has stored on your behalf must come to the surface, where you learn to face up to the responsibilities you have earned. That bitterness is the ego being fed its own demise.

Sometimes, this can be the stage when you tell all those people, with whom you have never been truthful with, what you really think of them. It can be when you tell your partner about the disappointments that you have long stored away in your hidden pantry (hidden in your mind).

It is a time where, as you earn this surrender you bow to yourself. This respect filters back into your cells, and you are learning to see up and into—not just looking at yourself, but into your self—which assists all your feelings to want to redeem the hidden freedom that has been trapped by your ego throughout your lifetime.

The rest of your internal organs now have the opportunity to begin their own cleansing process; they are the collectors of your co-existence. This is where we begin to accept the concordance of self. They must be adhered to, as this sets the patterns for the Divinity of death to congratulate itself.

Look back at those you have loved—and, in your own truth, you will remember what emotions they went through as they learned to accept their own destiny. I refer to Stage Two as the blame stage, where you empty your own cup by releasing the thoughts about why you blamed others for your own shortcomings. Once that is done, you have the opportunity to relook at the blame and reflect each thought back to yourself. You are entering back into your own educational university, where you are being reminded of your own shortcomings so that you can reshape your mind in order to begin again.

This is where we, as therapists, have the opportunity to come in and remind you that you now have the opportunity to construe your thinking; you will now be able to reinvest in yourself before the scales have tipped into their abundance. Your shock has been realized, and, when you come home to self-realization, you certainly have the opportunity to regenerate and begin again. The ego has sustained itself and is ready to listen. In other words, very simply, you have learned to surrender to you.

<u>If not, the story continues into Stage Three. The number three (3) in Sacred Numerology represents "the mind"</u>

Stage Three is the final stage of Death. This is where you are free to remind yourself that you have accepted death—that you are ready to surrender your greatest gift to God. This is where the ego submits, and you turn your life over. Stage Three occurs through your acceptance; you can willingly accept the inner freedom that the Soul releases.

Through the language of the Shamanic Inheritance, it is

known as the "applause we return to God".

Many people have released from the body in my arms. In most cases, their final words were, "Oh Wow! Look at the colours!" They each died with a smile on their faces. As death occurs, your energy moves up into the Collective Mind; this has opened up on your behalf and prepared a balanced mind for you prior to this moment. These colours are free to release, once your ego submits to your emotions, and they become the rainbow that naturally harmonizes the body in preparation for the passing from one world to the next. Think of the story of Joseph and his coat of many colours, which are explaining how the rainbow connection is released from within. The exchange of energy becomes easier through the mathematics arching throughout the body. Again, Einstein comes to mind through his explanation of the fields of relativity through time and space. We know that this creates gravity, so, in order for us to release our fields of gravity, we become eremitical—that is, the Soul absorbs our energy to bring us home to God. The more intellectually reformed you are (emotional intelligence), the easier the changeover.

There is no set time frame for those three stages, and not everyone goes through them in the same order (although the order of Stages One, Two, and Three as I have described them is the most typical). It depends entirely on how that person has lived up to their intelligence, and how he/she has accepted the merits of their inner wisdom prior to death.

The Soul cannot become trapped in the physical body; the body cannot surrender fully until the Soul has collected the life force and is ready to leave. It is only the last of the old fear that we have already created, through the innocence of our own belief, that is left in the body—and, it is those last remaining threads of our fear that keep us aware of our momentary surroundings.

The Soul is well above the body before the body stops breathing, so death is painless. It waits for the ego. Someone always comes to help us leave our layered garments (our body) behind—before we cross to the other side—always remember, we are never left to make the journey alone.

What happens when a person dies due to an accident?

If someone crosses over through the result of an accident, the ego—or fear of self—often echoes back through that person, until he/she can accept being in another dimension of time. The cause of his/her actions must release throughout the "scrolls of adjustment", which allows the memory to free itself. Such individuals do not carry on, day after day, in pain as many of you think. Someone always comes to help before we cross to the other side—always remember; we are never left to make the journey alone even in the case of accidents.

Our thinking causes accidents:

If only we all could understand this area more collectively, we would begin to realize that our thinking is our foremost priority—it is what allows us to theorize and release the Soul's evolution. This is also instigated throughout the whole of humanity; we set the wheels in motion not only for our own family, but also for the town or village that we live in. After which, it ventures out to the state, and then to the whole country, and we are obliquely designing how many deaths will occur for all humanity to bear. We are oblivious to the consequences of our own thinking, and yet, all the time, the mathematics of the Collective Consciousness still keeps adding up our thoughts.

What happens when family members pass over?:

When family members have passed over and reached the next dimension, they begin the transformational process. Their thoughts multiply through the Collective Consciousness, as they learn to equalize their mind, and carry themselves forward into the oneness. This is where thought attracts thought, energy attracts energy, time attracts time, and attention springs to attention. They begin to mirror their intelligence back into their reflective light as they enhance their freedom through the expediency they are earning.

For example, a member of your family dies. Five days later, Mrs. Smith from down the road comes up to you and says, "Your Bill came and saw me last night; he must have arrived safely, as it didn't take him too long to come back."

It is Bill's positive thinking in the hereafter that sparks his energy vibrations back here to the planet. He could return through Mrs. Smith, as she was sufficiently balanced in her mind to hear him. Because you were still in the grieving process, you could not hear him. When we spend our time grieving, our energy becomes heavier, and we miss the transformation process of helping our loved ones adjust into their new abode.

In consciousness, when we die, we automatically return to the source of all; and, through time as we know it here on the earth, we meld our mind, where we are able to facet our thoughts back into those whom we have left behind.

What happens to the genetic inheritance of the DNA?:
When one of you steps before me for consultation, your families who are still here, as well as the evolution of your DNA and those who have already passed over appear, all stand behind you. Although they have physically passed over, they are still permanently in the Collective Consciousness. Why? Through the fourth-dimensional thought form of time. Another explanation is that the results of your unconscious mind are free to release to me. This is the genetic inheritance of your DNA. As you were, so you shall live. Their previous experiences become your experiences, and the responsibility through all of this knowing, thus becomes yours. You are the channel for their success, and this then gives you the mind's right to evolve and expedite your own future.

When does the deceased person know what has happened to them?:
We refer to the afterlife by many other names: "dimensional time-shifting", "cellular recognition", "holographic imprints", and "parallel worlds", "heaven". The speed at which those who have passed over understand what has happened to them all depends on their belief in their emotional self, which is now the accumulation of their intellect. Everyone is accompanied on the transition by loving higher beings and are never alone.

What happens to the body when the Soul leaves?:
When the energy (Soul) leaves the body, that body begins its deterioration process. The energy of the light force of the planet overtakes the body, and it returns to the earth. If the

body is cremated, the energy of the fire consumes the body, which becomes ash; thus, the body, in turn, becomes the fire. The fire is the resurrection. If everyone understood those beautiful words, "Ashes to ashes, and dust to dust".

The unconscious/higher mind prepares us for a death three days prior:
When I counsel those who are grieving, I suggest that they go back and understand the conversations that they had with the deceased in their last few days. It is just amazing what we can remember. Those conversations, which could have been spoken or telepathically shared, represent the Metaphysical language releasing itself. The unconscious/higher mind prepares all parties concerned for the appropriate liaison that allows for the release. Even in the event of an accidental death, if you go back over the most recent conversations—especially your thoughts three days prior to the death—you will notice how the Collective was preparing you for this major event.

Do people come back to haunt us?:
No one who has died can ever come back to haunt us; we do that to ourselves through not listening to the messages of our own judicious (observant) wisdom. That goes for haunted houses as well. What we see from this experience is a message for you; it is not a message from the other side. The ego can play magnificent games to keep itself in control.

When I am in a half-sleep state at night, I see entities, and they seem very real to me. Why is that?:
It is the expansion of your own Soul. Your aura is the vibration that comes from your Soul, and those astral bodies manifest inside your aura. Astral bodies are symbolically formed through your thinking. When we are in that lucid dreaming state of mind, we are bordering between worlds. You are on the edge of allowing your mind to enter into the unconscious mind of the Collective Consciousness. You own 144,000 personalities (aspects of self) which live within that plane of unconscious energy and are manifesting through the worlds of your thinking. When you feel and see energies moving within, out of, and around your aura—or your Soul energy—once again, these are your own thoughts mirroring your story

back to you.

<u>Why do people commit suicide?:</u>
Let us now move to another subject in regard to a growing concern that seems to be a tortuous moment in people's lives: suicide. People commit suicide through being caught up emotionally as to a condition that has gone beyond their intellectual control; it is where they have become entangled in their fears of the moment.

They could see no way out.

I have had many interesting contacts who have spoken to me through the afterlife, in regards to their thoughts they had before they released their attitude of the moment. Notice how I am interpreting this story. They drove themselves to commit suicide through their anger collecting and creating itself through the consequences of not being able to reach beyond the boundaries of their mind. They felt hemmed in!

They became trapped through the thought of the moment repeating itself over and over again in their mind. This thought took control and blotted everything else out! Their deepest regret is the pain that they allowed others to feel on behalf of what they remember as their last and most important moment.

Please remember the Soul is well above the body before the body stops breathing, so death is painless. It awaits on the boundaries of the ego. Someone always comes to help us before we cross to the other side—always remember, we are never left to make the journey alone.

<u>When young children die:</u>
When young children die, we find that they can surrender very simply; they can accept their passing quite easily. The predicament begins to create itself when we, as parents, start mentally trying to call them back to us. We have had full responsibility of caring for and rearing this child, and it is quite natural for us to want to know where our child is going. Yes, we know our little one is journeying into heaven, and yes, we also know our little one is placed in God's arms. Now

add this information to your own portfolio, the children are well protected by the young beings of light who care and play with them as they grow up into their maturity of intelligence. Also don't forget the Grandmother's and grandfathers who shower them with love and cuddles, which gives the child their own sustenance in regards to a family life. Through our innocence, we want to be with our child; and, somewhere deep inside our thinking, we believe that our child has been cut short of his/her own existence. However, this is not so, as I can assure you having listened to hundreds of families release their stories through the experience of losing their child.

When you feel the child around you:
Many people have told me that they can feel their child around them after he/she has passed over. They may well feel that, but the child is not there to contact the parent, unless the child has something to say. Remember that, for the Soul to release, all must be mathematically equated correctly. Learn to still your mind and listen—you will see whether it is you calling for your child, or your child calling you. The child usually calls to inform you to stop grieving and get on with your life. Usually, those are the first words they speak when they have made contact with us. The realm that they have stepped into is full of rainbows and colours that you are not even aware of yet.

When an Elderly Life Partner Dies:
When an elderly life partner dies, the responsibility is then placed on the one who is left behind. The couple has been eating, sleeping, walking, and talking together for over fifty years, and, over that time, the temple that created their relationship has become as one. Which one of the two had the most Spiritual connection to themselves? The mathematics has been adjusted according to their Universal Laws for one of them to release. Look back to your own parents or grandparents to see which one had the greatest inner strength. Look to see which one surrendered, in order for the other to continue on and learn.

Elderly people sometimes ask, "Why am I still here?":
I have been inundated with elderly people asking me questions,

such as "Why am I still here?" "Why can't I die?" "Why will God not take me?" The most important one that they ask is when they reach towards me and say, "I have had enough. I have reared my children, and now they have theirs. I have lived my life, so what do I have to do before I die?" Gently, I coerce them into the teachings about how their family must birth their own intelligence and evolve before the parent can return home (pass over). Most of them are proud to take on the role of the Adept, and they are willing to find the courage and accept the challenge that is set before them. They now have time to rethink and understand their family, which turns to a deep love and respect for who they are as human beings.

What about keeping someone alive on a life-support system?: Hospitals realize the instant benefit of the life-support system, where, in the given moment, they can help a patient remember their service to themselves—although I would like you to think about this next equation, because, when this continues over a long period of time, it is time to rethink! When someone is put onto a life-support machine to postpone death, that machine takes over to extend that person's life force. While we are keeping someone alive against his/her Divine will, it interferes with the next step of the family's inheritance (DNA inheritance that is energetically passed on through death).

Death is just a new beginning. Understand, accept, and have the ability now to act out in freedom and joy for the rest of your life.

Appendix B—Remote Viewing And Astral Travelling

<u>Remote Viewing</u>
As we learn to open up the psyche, we are adjusting our levels of consciousness. In other words, we are travelling up into higher fields of intellect. We are learning to broaden our horizons where we are able to see more. This is relaxing and freeing up our DNA. We feel more relaxed as there is no pressure coming from our ego. It is up in the ethereal layers that our consciousness acquires extra information. If we are asking a question, automatically we are taken to that energy; our telepathic enhancement has directed us. In other words, it is through my Higher Self and the Higher Self of the energy collected that gives oneself permission to do so.

With remote viewing there is no interference; we are just standing beside them. It is as though we see through their eyes. I can vouch for this through my experiences in my police work connecting to murder cases, the information surprised me that I could be there in that given moment, to gather the information I needed and sitting in my office as well. In other words, I was in two places at once. It did not matter where on the planet the information was coming from; it was given to me in my moment. The event could have happened five minutes ago or ten, twenty or 150 years previously. Once we move beyond time, which is collated through the levels of the unconscious/higher mind, that moment is still there, somewhere embedded in the Collective Consciousness. There are no lies, no distortion; we are only given the natural law of truth as it occurred in that moment. Remote viewing all depends on your intellectual behaviour (emotional intelligence); it all depends on how much you respect and believe in self.

I often have people who are remote viewing appearing to see what I am doing or writing. I blank my mind and request them to leave. If they are listening to my lectures, I telepathically request that they keep to themselves and I honour them for what they are doing. Sometimes I would ask them to participate with the students, although rarely would they do so. Someone who is remote viewing and someone who has passed over have the same frequency—I am able to differentiate between the two with my third eye. It does not distort or lie.

Astral Travelling
Astral travelling and out-of-body-experiences are similar to remote viewing. The difference is that with astral travelling and out-of-body experiences, we gain "extra cities of Enlightenment" through the awareness of the unconscious mind, that we are able to use and walk into in reference to the subject at hand. The more we evolve, the more our astral bodies manifest themselves; we can have five or ten astral bodies working on our behalf at the same time. What we term "astral bodies" are symbolically formed through the multiplication of thoughts reaching their zenith, which manifest inside your auric fields. We learn to open and expand our thoughts through yoga, our dreams, tai chi or through any form of meditation; all of which brings harmony and balance to the mind. Through balancing your mind, you uplift your emotions, and you become aware of your emotional intelligence. This emotional intelligence is a reasoning of perpetual motion, which continuously balances and harmonizes your mind, body, and Soul. Remember that the astral plane varies on the intellect (emotional intelligence) that you have reached. There are many layers of consciousness, and this quest can take you a lifetime, and the time it takes depends entirely on the belief you can inherit within yourself.

Appendix C—Review Of Our Individual Universal Law And The Laws Of The Universe

Introducing our Individual Universal Law and the Laws of the Universe, excerpt from my book "Decoding the Laws of the Universe".

It is our own Individual Universal Law creating the Laws of the Universe! It is where we all become involved, and, through time and cause and effect, we have created and advanced our evolution for all humanity to inherit. The Laws of the Universe, (also known as the Universal Law, the God essence and many other terminology), is the Soul Energy of the Collective Consciousness; it is a mathematical program of all that is.

It is the Soul's purpose (each person) to be here on the planet, and each Soul must release and improve the energy that has collected from the past. We are asked to live and discover this inner truth that is embedded in the depths of the Laws of the Universe, which are embedded in each one of your cells. Our journey is to repair the thoughts of our previous generations as we journey forward which expedites their layers of confinement. Please remember, we have evolved for a very special reason.

Our own Individual Universal Law refers to the metaphysical philosophy that each individual is responsible for creating their own reality through their thoughts and emotional intelligence. The nature of each person's thinking, unique perspective and energy contributes to the overall consciousness of the universe. This knowledge is transformative on a personal level; once we understand, we can make great waves for all of humanity to inherit.

OVERVIEW:

<u>Our Individual Universal Law</u>
We are each our own Universe with our own Individual Universal Law, and we exist within a greater Universe that has its own proprietary law as well.

You are your own Universal Law; and, as you think, so, too, you create. You are given this gift to be in charge of how your thoughts create your world. As you allow one thought to finish itself, the next one is waiting to release itself to you. Your next thought will wait patiently until you are silent enough to allow it to come through.

Your Individual Universal Law is not created by what you do, but, rather, by your silent thoughts, regressions (thinking in the past), joys, frustrations, and peace. It is the energy and evolution of your emotional intelligence and how you connect to you. Once you understand what your Individual Universal Law is, keep yourself focused, and you will be able to fulfil all your desires. Life will bring you up, through the temperance of your Soul, and, when you can define this inner education, you will become and join forces with the Divine.

The Laws of the Universe
It is our Individual Universal Law creating the Laws of the Universe! It is where we all become involved, and, through time and cause and effect, we have created and advanced our evolution for all humanity to inherit. These Laws of the Universe are also known as the following: Collective Consciousness, Universal Law, the God essence, Collective Library of the Consciousness, World Consciousness, Collective Inheritance, Collective Memory, Collective Mind, Collective Soul of the God Force, Akashic Hall of Records, Hall of Recognition, Soul Energy of Collective Consciousness, and my favourite the, Eternal Matrix.

The Laws of the Universe (Collective Consciousness) registers all our conscious thinking, which must return to the conscious mind in order for our energy to continue to grow through the human evolution. The past from day one, is still alive in the Collective Consciousness; that Collective Inheritance is all of our thinking and evolution. We cannot forget yesterday, but we can absorb it; we can soak it up into our own consciousness and use it in the moment.

The Laws of the Universe answers to our thinking in a balanced way, although, it is not always in the way that we expect it to be! Another name for it is Karma, or the "Kha-Rha-Mha", if we explain it correctly, for this goes back to the early language of the Armenians and the hieroglyphs of Egypt. If we pronounce it in its correctness, it is the cause and effect, or the accidental and occidental; it is the occidental that is the key to your wisdom. The occidental is the final outcome of the length of your stay on this planet. The occidental is the light that keeps this planet alive.

So, your knowledge of these secrets can carry you to the place where you have the opportunity to dance along with these Laws of the Universe. As you begin to believe in yourself, your Soul gives you never-ending gifts of knowledge. To believe in yourself takes a tremendous amount of courage for you to release, and that courage will lead you into other parallel worlds of existence. Those worlds align within and open you up to your inner worlds, where you have earned the freedom to use them to promote your tomorrows.

EXPLAINED FURTHER—DELVING DEEPER:

<u>Our Individual Universal Law</u>
Let us explore further, our own Individual Universal Law. As stated previously your Individual Universal Law is not created by what you do, but, rather, by your silent thoughts, regressions (thinking in the past), joys, frustrations, and peace. It is the energy and evolution of your emotional intelligence and how you connect to you.

Understanding and connecting with our emotional intelligence is key to tapping into our Individual Universal Law. This involves becoming aware of our thoughts, of our emotions, learning to identify and process them, and understanding the ways in which they influence our actions, and outcomes we experience in life. By paying attention to the patterns and themes that emerge in our lives, we can begin to identify the underlying beliefs and values that shape our perceptions of reality.

Our emotional intelligence is instrumental to the evolution of our Individual Universal Law. Our emotions are energy in motion, and they have a vibrational frequency that attracts experiences and circumstances of a similar frequency. When we are in a positive emotional state, we are vibrating at a higher frequency, and we tend to attract positive experiences and people into our lives. Conversely, when we are in a negative emotional state, we are vibrating at a lower frequency, and we tend to attract negative experiences and people into our lives.

Therefore, to evolve our Individual Universal Law and attract more positive experiences into our lives, it is crucial to work on our emotional intelligence and maintain a positive emotional state as much as possible. This means being aware of our emotions, expressing them in healthy ways, and choosing to focus on positive emotions such as love, gratitude, joy, and a feeling of peace with oneself. We can use mindfulness, staying in the moment and have an awareness of the chatter of the mind.

You can also examine your "relationship of self". Your relationship of self is the way you relate to you. It is created by the thoughts you have about yourself, belief in self, the emotions you feel about yourself, your judgements about yourself, your perception your self-worthiness and how you honour yourself—your internal dialogue to self. When your belief in self builds upon its own strength and creates your next positive thought, your life becomes so much easier for you to manage.

How can we improve our relationship with ourselves, and what steps can we take to cultivate a more positive internal dialogue that supports our self-belief and self-worth? How can we break free from negative thought patterns and judgments about ourselves, and build a stronger foundation of self-love and self-acceptance and discipline, that empowers us to create a more fulfilling life? How can we identify and change limiting beliefs that may be holding us back, and replace them with more empowering beliefs that support our growth and development? The answer is by cultivating a positive internal dialogue. Improving our relationship with ourselves involves several steps. Firstly, we need to become aware of our current internal dialogue and how we communicate to ourselves. We can start by observing our thoughts and emotions, and noticing any patterns of negativity or self-judgment. Once we have identified these patterns, we can work on changing them by replacing negative self-talk with positive self-talk and affirmations of "I believe in myself". To cultivate a more positive internal dialogue, we can furthermore practice self-compassion and self-forgiveness. To break free from limiting beliefs and judgments about ourselves, we can challenge these beliefs and reframe them in a more positive and empowering light. This can involve seeking out new perspectives and information, and exploring new ways of thinking and being. When your belief in self builds upon its own strength and creates your next positive thought, watch how the miracles manifest in your life where you will find you are continuously working as one with the universe.

This journey is yours and cannot be given to anyone else; the responsibility is yours alone. The hierarchical mind/unconscious mind/higher mind, also known as the Higher Self, will always be there to step in front of you, protecting and holding you firmly when you cannot believe or when you have lost your trust in you. Our Higher Self is a deeper and evolved aspect of our being and has access to higher levels of wisdom, intuition, and guidance. Our Higher Self, presents experiences for us. It gives us the opportunity for our thoughts to repeat throughout our life until we can find the strength to overcome them. This suggests that our Higher Self may be trying to teach us something or help us grow by presenting recurring negative thoughts, experiences, or fears.

Our thinking can create our fear in the moment by the way we perceive and interpret our experiences, this leads on to attracting Depression! Our thoughts and beliefs regarding a current situation can trigger a fear response in our body, even if there is no actual physical threat. Our thoughts can also create a negative feedback loop, where the fear response reinforces the negative thinking, leading to more fear and anxiety. By changing our thinking and challenging our beliefs, we can break this cycle and reduce our fear and anxiety in the moment.

If you find yourself repeatedly experiencing negative thoughts, fears, or experiences, it is important to stop them before they become greater. Remember the traffic lessons you learned in school: stop, look, and listen. Take a moment to search beyond the present moment and see how this energy or thought is recreating itself. To search beyond the present moment, is to take a step back and analyse the situation objectively.

One way to do this is to observe the thoughts and feelings that arise when the negative thought, experience or fear resurfaces. Ask yourself questions such as: What triggered this thought or feeling? What emotions am I experiencing? Is there a pattern to these thoughts and feelings? Reflect on how this thought or fear has impacted your life and try to gain insight into why it keeps coming back. This process of self-reflection can help you identify the underlying causes of the negative thought or fear and find ways to overcome it. This is not a learning experience, but an earning experience.

The difference between the two is that learning means "looking at" something, while earning means "looking through" it. Your Higher Self, presents these experiences to you as an opportunity to overcome them. One thing in life is certain: You cannot run away from yourself. There is nowhere to hide! You create your fear in the moment through your thinking. Write this down: "My fear is created by me, as I am refusing to live and accept this Divine moment in my life." By acknowledging your power over your thoughts, you can take the first step towards personal transformation.

If I can help you to understand and accept, where you can act out your thoughts through self-confidence and assurance; then we are both winners. Hopefully you will have the opportunity to rake away your fears, as this is the sole—and Soul—reason for you to be here, and it is what this life's quest is all about. We rake up all the leaves after the autumn season has ended, and we prepare the garden for winter. Winter is the time for hibernation, and it is through our own hibernation that we are given the time to dichotomize, which means to sort out right from wrong and refrain from making the same mistakes.

When we look out our window again, our garden looks tidy and free; the raking has allowed it to regain its own silence and to breathe new life as it prepares to birth itself for the next season.

For years in the journey to discover this metaphysical knowledge (that is, before I became an Adept in the Secrets of the Universal Laws), I went into the "Worlds of Invisible Kingdoms" (explored other dimensions) and was asked by my teachers to read the Bible in the reverse from Revelations back to Genesis, instead of the other way around. It is not necessary for you to do this. My teachers informed me that, by doing this, I could bring through a resonance of intelligence that all of humanity could view from within themselves—where they could understand the capabilities of how their intelligence unfolds itself, and then that knowledge would be available for them to add to what they had already achieved. "Why?" I asked my teachers. "Your program fits the bill" they told me. "What program?" I persisted. "The thoughts of your previous generations have been indelibly imprinted in you, and you have made yourself available; you asked, so now you have the opportunity to receive!" That's what they told me!

To further explain, a "life program". Your life program was created through your parents' DNA, which provided the basic principles for you to become you. Your task is to unfold yourself through the disadvantages of your parents' judgment and through their innocence in (mis)understanding themselves! You have chosen to live what your parents were too afraid to face through their acceptance of self as they understood it, and, more importantly, you have also chosen to live their gains.

Your life program keeps on creating itself through each of your thoughts building upon the other, and the transformation continues until you have taken your last breath. That energy force field grows in strength and opens you up into your Higher—or heavenly—Self. That Higher Self follows you through every thought you think, always encouraging you to create and expand your thinking.

To carry your DNA inheritance into your next step of humanity's earnings is how and why you have evolved to be here, through balancing and clearing your past generations' thinking and programming the basics of the mind of your future generations. Once we have accepted this program, it is no longer a detriment to your consciousness; the freedom you create in your mind will allow your intelligence to have the ability to evolve even further. Once we have recognized and solved the tasks that have been given to us by our genetic inheritance, we are free to collect more information to add to the benefits available to us beyond this program.

During those years of my internal searching, my intelligence grew into the "Wisdom of the Sages", where I could see through the layers of restriction that I had hidden behind for my own protection. I also began to study the science behind humanity's thinking, and, as this information grew, understanding it fully became my ultimate goal; as a result, over the years, all knowledge consumed me. I found I could unite the plumber with the librarian, the lawyer with the builder, the electrician with the social worker, and then unite them all into a whole! It is the relationship of self that connects us to the energy of our total evolution. This knowledge has grown stronger and stronger over the last thirty years of my life. Subsequently, I brought all this information into a format that is ongoing in every moment of my life. I learned how to transfer this knowledge into the human body by beginning with just one cell.

Once you understand what your Individual Universal Law is, keep yourself focused, and you will be able to fulfil all your desires. To keep ourselves focused and fulfil our desires according to our Individual Universal Law, we need to maintain a clear and positive mindset. This means consistently monitoring our thoughts and redirecting any negative or limiting beliefs towards positive and empowering ones. We can do this by practicing mindfulness and being present in the moment, observing our thoughts and choosing to let go of any that do not serve us. Visualization and affirmations can also be powerful tools to help us stay focused and aligned with our desired outcomes. By visualizing ourselves already having achieved our goals and repeating positive affirmations that affirm our abilities and worthiness to receive what we desire, we can tap into the power of our Higher Self and attract more of what we want into our lives. Life will bring you up, through the temperance of your Soul, and, when you can define this inner education, you will become the Laws of the Divine.

The Laws of the Universe

Let us explore further The Laws of the Universe. As stated, it is our Individual Universal Law creating the Laws of the Universe! It is where we all become involved, and, through time and cause and effect, we have created and advanced our evolution for all humanity to inherit. The Laws of the Universe (Collective Consciousness) registers all our conscious thinking, which must return to the conscious mind in order for our energy to continue to grow through the human evolution. The past is still alive in the Collective Consciousness; that Collective Inheritance is all of our thinking and evolution. We cannot forget yesterday, but we can absorb it; we can soak it up into our own consciousness and use it in the moment.

The Collective Consciousness registers all our conscious thinking by storing and recording every thought, emotion, and experience in a universal database or energy field. It is the energy of the thought, emotion, and experience that registers with the Collective Consciousness on a quantum level. Basically, explained on a quantum level, our thought energy interacts with the universe through the observer effect. This effect describes how the act of observation can change the behaviour of particles and systems in the universe. When we focus our thoughts on something, we are essentially observing it with our consciousness, and this observation can affect the behaviour of particles and systems related to that thing. According to quantum physics, all particles and systems in the universe are interconnected and entangled. This means that our thoughts and intentions can have an impact on the behaviour of these interconnected particles and systems. Our thoughts and emotions emit energy waves that can influence the energy of the Laws of the Universe, the Collective Consciousness. (The physical particle-like structure of matter existing in time-space, in which it exists non-locally "encoded" as a wave frequency in the past, present and future of the Collective Consciousness—the holographic universe).

This collective inheritance of knowledge and wisdom is available to us all and can be tapped into for personal growth and evolution. (Time-space reality is the frequency domain of the Higher Mind as well as the Collective Consciousness). As individuals contribute their thoughts and experiences to the collective, the database expands and evolves, contributing to the evolution of humanity as a whole.

The Laws of the Universe answers to our thinking in a balanced way, although, it is not always in the way that we expect it to be! Another name for it is Karma, or the "Kha-Rha-Mha", if we explain it correctly, for this goes back to the early language of the Armenians and the hieroglyphs of Egypt. If we pronounce it in its correctness, it is the cause and effect, or the accidental and occidental. It is the occidental that is the key to your wisdom. The occidental is the final outcome of the length of your stay on this planet. The occidental is the light that keeps this planet alive. That gift from the All That Is, is our attainment, and it is also how we have produced our next moment. Weather patterns, dis-eases, viruses, and wars are all creations of the atmospheric conditions of the Collective Consciousness; they are the results of the thinking of this planet. Our accidents are what we have produced for ourselves through our thinking. The occidental is the explanation, as to how we have gathered and achieved the accident in the first place. It is not only what you have done to you; it is how the Laws of the Universe answer back to what you are doing to you. I like to refer to the occidental as the "messenger" represented as the Pigeon throughout the Laws of Shamanism. With its sonic sound, it homes in on a catastrophic conclusion of thought, and then it delivers the message to our heavenly home, which is our brain.

Appendix D—Brief Metaphysical Overview Of The Brain/Mind/Levels of Consciousness

We have many different levels of consciousness that are available to us as we grow into our new relationship of self. As our intelligence releases itself from our bone matter, we are able to access these layers of new found "grace", which empowers our inner self, where it evolves throughout our language to reform into the word beauty. Throughout the Laws of Shamanism, we are gifted with the species of the swan in the creation of the human brain, as this species represents the waters, (the Collective Consciousness), known to us in the beginning as the emotion, grace, where we are able to sense and feel how to slide or glide our way through the endowment of self-acclaim. We are also gifted with each species of animal, vegetable, mineral, earth, the waters or the sky (all endowed with an emotion of energy in both negative and positive form), which is created throughout the evolution of the human brain during the first three months of human gestation. We class this as the ninety-day sentience, as our brain is superseded with every species that has earned its own vocabulary to live in our domain.

Our brain has two hemispheres—two parts. The left-brain is our logic (conscious mind). The left-brain is our masculine side; our ego, our primal fear, and as stated our logic. It portrays how we are representing ourselves to others through releasing from our next thought, as it can only register thirteen words per minute. It is also known as the child within. It still has to grow and mature into the adult phase. This hemisphere only looks at! It has difficulties to look through where it can view the whole picture as in its natural form it does not have the endowed intellect to understand as it is still too afraid to take the journey into the unknown.

The right brain is our emotions (subconscious mind). The right brain is our feminine side, our inner creative language. We give out to others with the right side, where our energy in motion—or emotion—creates itself from how we are giving and receiving to and from the self. The right brain represents what we are doing to ourselves within, and what we are capable of receiving through ourselves.

The people who live in their logical ego sense are perfect, and so, too, are the people who live in their creative emotional sense. In understanding the logical sense, we understand through our primal inheritance, where it begins to fit with common sense. The mind of logic is the echo from whatever is created, and it is also, what we attract in our outer worlds; the emotional mind sits within and takes care of our sense of responsibility.

We cannot survive on this planet without both ego and emotions. Our journey is to learn how to balance both brains so that we may advance our awareness of the supportiveness of our unconscious mind or Higher Self, (also known as the supra-consciousness, higher mind, ultra consciousness etc.). The unconscious/higher mind is the freedom with which we can tune into ourselves, but only when the other two parts of our brain have balanced through our attitude to our self. The unconscious/higher mind is the highest realm of our intellect, which mathematically measures, every thought that we think (mathematically measuring the inner balance of the mind, to build-up the energy of thought. Mathematics is the equation of cause and effect).

It has taken us a few years to come to terms with the intelligence of the unconscious mind. We have always been aware of it, but we do not quite understand it. We are becoming more aware of its intellect as we open up our own intelligence with each positive inner step we take. The unconscious mind is communicating through us, twenty-four hours a day, and, slowly, we are becoming aware of the advanced language of how it communicates back to us.

If we like to take this further, our left-brain, our conscious self, is firstly recognised as the child within, it is responsible for the first and second-dimensional mind. Our right brain, our subconscious self; is responsible for the third dimension and the relationship to the introduction into the fourth dimension, which relates to time. The balance of both brains through looking into one another, is when we enter into the doorway which delivers us up into our unconscious mind, which allows it to be responsible for the "temple of self" where we have earned the responsibility to live up to its expectations. Temple of self means we are training our self, moment by moment, to have control over our thinking. Our unconscious/higher mind is the make-up of our Divine Inheritance—or the language of our Soul—it is when we have earned our spiritual life force. The unconscious/higher mind is the world of telepathic communication.

Appendix E—Releasing The Past and Fears

<u>Clearing the Past—Stop stepping back in the past</u>
Do not become bogged down in the past; that song you sung is over. Stay in the moment, as that moment is a reflection of how your future must walk towards you. When your emotions become bogged down, do not speak them, just be aware of them; make note of them, and watch how they begin to accept this new you. Address the situation in the moment, and watch that moment disappear into the next one, and then, as you begin to ascend, all those emotions have also become aware of your strategy and through your confidence in self, they learn to become one.

It creates a feeling of worthiness that you are clearing past thoughts that are inhibiting your next advancement and the self-realisation of your inner Royal-ness. It's like house work, as they are layers of old limitation; please remember the old saying, a tidy house is a tidy mind. Focus now is on your responsibility of your thoughts to create your life, which is based on your opinion of self. It can't work while you have repetitious thoughts based on past limitations. Clearing ones past generations' thinking can prove to be an exemplified, or maybe a personified evolutionary journey, which is even closer to the beat of your heart.

<u>How does one stop stepping back into the past?</u>
Until you are prepared to take that first step forward, the Laws of the Universe will help you to your own expectations; although the moment you put your right foot forward, is the moment when the doors will open wider. Then you must keep on moving, without re-creating that old thought or fear. You will know when you are ready for each new step of your journey; your light within will then open new possibilities and show you the way. You will notice that your depressed mind that is embedded in past experiences and thoughts, begins to fade away!

An awareness grows from our own unique thoughts, sensations, memories, ideas, attitudes and beliefs. It is a sense of one's personal collective identity. Anything that we are aware of at any moment of time, forms part of our consciousness, and becomes our life force. (Consciousness refers to an individual "sense of self" or "inner-self").

Consciousness builds on consciousness. We often have a stream of consciousness—the flow of thoughts from our conscious mind. Our consciousness develops itself, one layer over another, similar to thin layers of silk—all the layers are an active force of energy. Our consciousness grows and matures which connects from these layers.

So, what is stopping you from moving forward? That same memorial experience or thought that you have already lived? Is it created back into your thinking again? Therefore, what is your next move? You, must stop it before it becomes greater, where it is given the opportunity to reinvest in itself again. I still remember my traffic lessons when I went to school: stop, look, and listen. Try to search beyond the moment to see how this energy or thought re-created itself. It is not a learning experience; this time, it becomes an earning. Are you aware of how you have accrued your mind? Please get out your Thesaurus, look up the word and find out which word suits you.

There is a big difference between learning and earning: the former means "looking at" which ignites your ego and the later means "looking through". Our Higher Self—our unconscious/ higher mind—presents all of these experiences for us. It gives us the opportunity for our thoughts to repeat throughout our life, until we can find the strength to overcome them. One thing in life is certain: You cannot run away from yourself. There is nowhere for you to hide!

Also review your dreams. We usually begin dreaming from midnight through to 2 a.m. Those dreams represent the torment that we have created for ourselves, from our past thinking. In dreams, our Higher Self (unconscious/higher mind) informs you that there is something you must release in your mind as your current thinking is choked up with unnecessary chatter; there is something of the past that you must bring up and rectify. For instance, if you are sacrificing to the self (doing things for others and receiving no benefit for self or trying to avoid responsibility for ourselves), that sacrifice will keep you embedded back into your past. Release can be found in the act of humbling self to one's Higher Self. When you have accepted these tokens of remembrance, you can thank the experience in order to free yourself and move forward.

Clearing Fear
Your thoughts are heard right around this planet. The Collective Consciousness sonically registers them. You must remember that your fear, as well as your expectations, creates your reality.

Understand that your fear is with you at all times—until you have earned the freedom in the mind to allow it to release itself. Up to that point, your fear is your driving force, and we cannot live without it, while you are learning to trust your own mind. That fear is your ego rebounding back into its own self-acclaim, where it creates its own quandary. Although, through you accepting your inner equation—or the responsibility that you now understand regarding self—you can see how it manipulates your well-being and how it wants to seize your mind and regain control.

Find the strength to love your own insecurities—your fear, which is the child within us all. That child must grow up—or spiral up—into becoming the adult. The word "spiral" refers to the place where you have the opportunity to turn around and accept our self, at the exact moment when the positive energy steps forward to offer itself to you.

On your life's journey, you will die to, and grow away, from your old ways of thinking. Through your own assertion, you will learn to release your fear through finding enough courage, strength, and power to believe that you are a miracle (a "mirror of your cells").

Always listen to your thoughts. You create your fear in the moment through your thinking. An affirmation to help: "I release my fear and I live and accept this Divine moment in my life."

It was the little things that I began to understand at first, I discovered how to release the pressures of my past that had a hold on me—at last, through my awareness, I could see how my past had tried to control me. For me to attain the Avatar education in my reality was phenomenal; there were years when I felt like I was trapped in an iron lung and had great difficulties learning to breathe; as my intellect slowly released itself from the core of my bones. For years my body ached inside me, as I learned to release the fear that I had inherited through the embedment of my DNA. And yet there was another side to the journey I had undertaken and that was of pure bliss for me to release my inner freedom. Many times, I felt like I was ten feet tall. As my cosmic force fields extended; which is my auric fields of intellectual attainment I knew that there was nothing the universe could present to me, to keep me embedded in my fear. It is similar to the astronauts adjusting their breathing apparatus when they are out in the ether, floating around in space.

If we do not allow our intelligence to release, we begin to walk backwards, which is where those negative thoughts that are our own emotional blockages, create a depressed state of mind, as they can lead us into going back over the same steps we have just achieved; this knowing sets the pathway of depression to build upon its self, which creates the destruction towards our futuristic abilities. We are walking away from what we are innocently aiming for. We lack the judgement to discern the responsibility to earn, which allows our fear to suspend us.

I have been informed that George Lucas, the creator of "Star Wars", undertook training under the guidance of the late brilliant author Joseph Campbell, who wrote more than sixty books and gave us a wealth of information that he had gathered from around the world regarding the "Masks of God'. When George Lucas had gathered his information, he sat down and wrote the magnificent "Star Wars" series that is still so popular today. All his movies can be taken as exercises explaining the emotional personalities (aspects) of the mind, and these personalities are just a spark of what is in each human to view for him/herself. Luke Skywalker had to find his strength in order to release his light, and he did so through overcoming the dark force—Darth Vader. The secret of the movie came that at the end, when Luke found out that the dark force was really his father. In other words, he had the responsibility of clearing his past evolution—or DNA—of its own negativity, and only then was he free to collect what he needed to experience for himself.

Review your dreams—Sleep is needed for our ego—the ego being the world that houses and controls our fear. It is through sleep that the unconscious/higher mind can return to us the results of our thinking. Therefore, we must accept the responsibility for our own thoughts as they are presented back to us. Those dreams come to us in a metaphysical resonance; they are delivered back to us in the form of a riddle or a parable as stated previously. We have to work the meaning of each dream out in our mind.

Dreams also manifest from the stories of our past generations, if our higher mind thinks that we are regaining (using) the same excuse as our ancestor lived. Those excuses are the fears that are instilled in us when our past generations did not understand or overcome their own excuses. Therefore, those dreams bank up in every forthcoming generation.

When we are aware of and can decipher our dreams, we free up not only our own fear but also the fear of our past generations. When you are lying in bed and going to sleep you shut down the conscious self (left brain/ego), then you open up the subconscious self (right brain/emotions) and release the unconscious/higher mind, this world of silence, will be knowable to us and we will know where we are heading. We are participating on this journey of wanting to know what is up above, but the old stuff holds us back. So, now you should be able to understand how so much of your fear has been created.

Our reality is already created for us when we are born, through the thoughts of the mother's ninety days before gestation and also within the first three months of gestation, and by our genetic inheritance. This is your foundation. Therefore, you are born with the foundations of reality on the thoughts of both parents. For example, a son would grow up like the father because he reflected the emotional hiccups that the father had.

A foundational reality is already set, and then it is up to you how we learn to understand who we are. The Natural Law is of who you are and that is your challenge to become who you wish to be. What are your desires? How do you wish to define yourself? You have the ability to overcome, to step forward to release your inner fears. Those thoughts that you think, are they holding you back? You have the right to step forward as your our intellect unfurls.

For those of you who know yourselves, your thoughts are the creation of dreams for the rest of humanity, all through you understanding yourselves. Congratulations on every one of your futuristic endeavours.

Notes:

Books By O.M. Kelly (Omni)

Decoding The Mind Of God
Author O.M. Kelly's seminal work, "Decoding the Mind of God", is a compilation of nine volumes of metaphysical information based on the research into the coded information of the Laws of the Universe, also known as the Collective Consciousness, and represents a groundbreaking contribution to our understanding of the metaphysical universe. Now, all nine volumes are being released as separate, revised books, each offering a unique perspective on the universe's workings. Omni's work has been widely acclaimed for its depth of insight, and her contributions to the field of metaphysics have been groundbreaking.
The nine separate volumes encompassing:

The Laws of the Universe
Thought
Dis-Ease
Death
Sexuality and Spirituality
The Dolphin's Breath
Sacred Alphabet and Numerology
Sacred Fung Shwa
Extra-Terrestrial Intelligence.
Updated version of each book now being released separately.

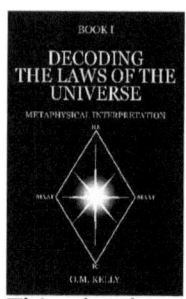

Book I. Decoding The Laws Of The Universe
If you're looking to unlock the hidden potential within you and transform your life, "Decoding the Laws of the Universe" is the book for you. This powerful and insightful book is designed to help you understand the deeper, metaphysical aspects of life and tap into the transformative power of the universe utilising the secrets of our Individual Universal Law.
This book serves to introduce you into the secrets of our Individual Universal Law. This amazing knowledge and wisdom, is transformative on a personal level and creates the opportunity for you to interrelate with the Laws of the Universe. Throughout this book, you will dive deep into the inner workings of your mind and discover the hidden laws that govern your life. You will learn about the alchemy of the mind and how to harness its power to create positive change in your life and the world around you. Through the lens of Metaphysical philosophy, you will gain a new perspective

on the world and your place in it. You will learn how the universe communicates with you through coded intelligence and how to unlock the hidden messages that are all around you.

This book is a journey for personal transformation and spiritual growth. Take a voyage of exploration of the expansive vistas of information discovering the codes of Metaphysics and the Quest of Life. You will learn the Metaphysical coded wisdom of the ancients for the necessary mind elements to transit into a higher mindset. Explore the secret relationship between the Earth and human beings, the higher mind, the Metaphysical journey, the importance of self, belief in self, the codes of mythology, a higher level of attainment, releasing the past, fears and evolving one's light on a Metaphysical level, what causes stress, work place promotion and why it does not happen, and many other topics. Included is a short overview of the conventional Twelve Laws of the Universe.

Book II. Decoding Thought
Welcome to a journey of self-discovery and exploration of the mysteries of the universe. "Decoding Thought" is a ground-breaking book that explores the power of the mind and the principles of metaphysical thought. Through a deep exploration of the mind and body connection, the author provides readers with insights to unlock the full potential of their thoughts. This book provides a guide to harnessing the power of the mind to create the life you desire. With explanations of metaphysical principles, the book makes these often complex concepts accessible to readers. "Decoding Thought" takes you on a journey through the vast landscape of the human mind. Explore the mysteries of thought power, and how it can shape our reality and transform our lives. The power of thought is not just a theoretical concept. It is a tangible force that can be harnessed to bring about significant changes in our lives.

This book can expand your consciousness and open your mind to new possibilities. By exploring the metaphysical principles that underlie our existence, you can gain a new perspective on life and the world around you. This book provides through a metaphysical interpretation explanations into the various aspects of thought power, including how it is linked to our DNA, and the roles played by the pituitary and pineal glands in our thought processes. O.M. Kelly also explains the metaphysical language in reference to the codes of the Egyptian Philosophies, the Bible, myths, cultures, and how they connect to the power of thought. The journey continues with a deep dive into the inner Secret School of Metaphysics, where we discover the Alchemy of the Brain and the pathway to our truth. Discover the unconscious/higher mind, and our Life Quest, which opens the doors to the Psychometric Consciousness. Through the lens of metaphysical interpretation, you will gain a new perspective on the impact of thought on our mental and emotional states that includes a look at Depression, Coping with Change and how to retrain our brain patterns to be positive and moving forward for our Financial Abundance and manifesting prosperity. The book ends with a brief overview of the brain/mind, and a short Q&A on thought power. This metaphysical book on the power of thought is a guide to discovering your true potential and creating the life you desire.

"Decoding Thought" is a must-read for anyone seeking to unlock the full potential of their mind and harness the power of the universe to create a life of fulfilment and this book serves as an invaluable resource.

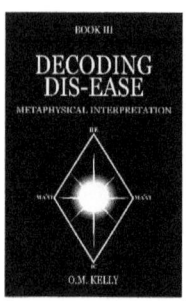

Book III. Decoding Dis-Ease

Introducing "Decoding Dis-Ease" a Metaphysical Interpretation into understanding the intricate web of factors that contribute to our health and well-being. From the author of several groundbreaking works on the interaction of the mind and body, this book delves into a wide range of topics related to dis-ease. It is a fascinating and insightful book that offers a fresh perspective on health and healing. It is a must-read for anyone interested in the mind-body connection.

Readers will be inspired to embark on a quest of discovering the codes within themselves, recognizing that every cell in our body is pure Cosmic Consciousness. They will also gain a deeper understanding of specific health topics such as the thyroid, the kidneys, men's problems, and many other topics from a Metaphysical perspective. The book also examines how a dis-ease is given to us in group energy and the complex interplay between our bodies and minds, and how every human has the consequences of all that we do and experience.

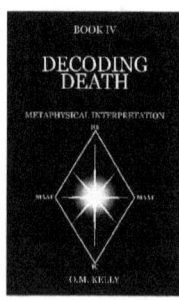

Book IV. Decoding Death

Looking for a thought-provoking exploration of death and the afterlife? Look no further than O.M. Kelly's book, "Decoding Death".

"Decoding Death takes us on a transformative Metaphysical journey through the mysteries of the Universe. O.M. Kelly—known as Omni—provides an expanded horizon of possibilities, awareness, and a transformative perspective. In this book, Omni delves into a wide range of topics related to dying and death, from the loss of a loved one to a viewing of the afterlife. Omni has a unique ability to view the Laws of the Universe using her extraordinary state of heightened awareness and multi-dimensional perception and through the lens of metaphysics offers a unique perspective on the nature of death and what it means for the human experience.

Omni shares personal experiences and stories, including the passing of her late husband, brother, and parents, and offers a metaphysical insight for those dealing with loss and grief. She explores the transformational process of death and the potential for spiritual growth and enlightenment. The book explains that the human experience of death is part of a larger Universal process that is ultimately guided by a higher intelligence referred to as God (Laws of the Universe/Collective Consciousness) or whatever name you prefer. Omni's exploration of death is both metaphysically comprehensive and thought-provoking, offering readers a deep and nuanced understanding of one of life's greatest mysteries. With chapters on the Three Doorways—Three Stages of Death, The Quantum Hologram—Why a partner dies for the other partner to progress in the "Journey of Life", The Passing to the Afterlife, and many other enlightening chapters, "Decoding Death" offers a unique viewpoint. By drawing on a range of religious, philosophical, and metaphysical perspectives, Omni offers a compelling vision of the human experience of death and its role in the larger Universal Law.

Book V. Decoding Sexuality And Spirituality

Welcome to "Decoding Sexuality and Spirituality" by O.M. Kelly. In this book, explore the fascinating relationship between our sexuality and spirituality, and how these two aspects of ourselves are intimately intertwined. Delve into the concept that sexuality is the doorway to our spirituality, and examine the powerful and transformative energy that is generated when we fully embrace our sexual selves. The book also explores the notion of the metaphysical orgasmic cloud, and how it can be used to deepen our connection to our spiritual selves. We will also examine the role of marriage in our sexual and spiritual lives.

For women, the book offers a unique perspective on the journey of embracing sexuality and spirituality, as well as insights into the different stages of life and how they impact our sexual and spiritual selves. Drawing on both ancient wisdom traditions and metaphysical mythology, the book examines the myth of Hercules and how it relates to our sexual intelligence. By decoding the symbolism of this myth, we can gain a deeper understanding of the ways in which our sexuality and spirituality intersect and influence each other. So if you are ready to embark on a journey of self-discovery and unlock the true potential of your sexual and spiritual selves, then "Decoding Sexuality and Spirituality" is the book for you.

VI. Decoding The Dolphin's Breath

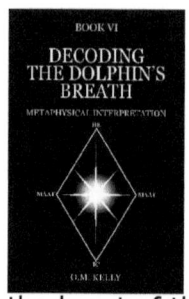

"Decoding The Dolphin's Breath" by O.M. Kelly (Omni) is a captivating exploration of the relationship between humans and dolphins. The book begins with a poignant account of a real-life encounter between the author and a group of wild dolphins, setting the stage for a deep dive into the spiritual and metaphysical significance of dolphins. This captivating book takes readers on a journey into the heart of the dolphin-human relationship, exploring the ways in which these majestic creatures can help us attune to the power of free will, and telepathic communication.

Throughout the Laws of Shamanism the wonderful Dolphin in consciousness, represents the attainment we can reach through ourselves earning our freedom of will. This book explains the benefits of the dolphins breath—the why and how we use the breath that influences our divine mentality. Further, it's a story which reveals how the dolphins have taught us the process to be free of fear, and to tap into the Language of Babylon—to understand the language of Earth. One of the key themes of the book is the idea that dolphins are always breathing their total freedom of thought, and the author provides insights into how humans can learn from this remarkable trait. The book also invites readers to embark on a journey into understanding the telepathic communication of whales and dolphins. Inclusive in the book is a written meditation which assists you to connect to the external consciousness and release the fear that you have wrapped around yourself for protection.

Overall, this book offers a unique and fascinating perspective on the metaphysics of dolphins, and will appeal to anyone interested in spirituality, and the power of the mind.

Book VII. Decoding The Sacred Alphabet And Numerology

This book offers a myriad of explanations concerning the higher consciousness in relationship to names, places and numbers. "Decoding The Sacred Alphabet & Numerology" by O.M. Kelly (Omni) is a thought-provoking and enlightening read that

offers a unique perspective on the metaphysical world of letters and numbers.

Omni's insights and teachings are sure to inspire readers to deepen their understanding of the ancient sacred codes to names of places, your name and the sacred alphabet. The author also delves into the practice of metaphysical numerology, which involves using numerical values to interpret personality traits, life paths, and other aspects of a person's life. Omni explains how metaphysical numerology can be used to gain insight into our spiritual path and to better understand our purpose in life. Your ability to decipher the Sacred Alphabet and Numerology codes commonly and constantly presented to you throughout your life, will open opportunities to expand your consciousness and awareness you never thought possible.

Embark on a journey through the myth of Babylon and Shambhala and discover the sacred language that connects us all. Explore Luxor, the Delta Giza Saqqara and Faiyum, and Solomon's Temple, and uncover the mysteries of Akhenaton and Tomb KV-63. Find out how to unravel the threads of your DNA and unlock the ancient knowledge of the Old Aramaic Story of Aladdin and the Lamp. Explore Grecian stories through the Metaphysical language and travel along the Old Silk Road. Discover the Shamanic inheritance of numbers and their meanings, and learn how we rely on numbers to read the hidden language of the universe. Join O.M. Kelly on a journey of self-discovery and uncover the divine language within.

Book VIII. Decoding Sacred Fung Shwa

Introducing "Decoding Sacred Fung Shwa", the revolutionary guide to understanding and harnessing the energy within your home and yourself. In this book, author O.M. Kelly (Omni), has introduced a metaphysical sixth element that takes our understanding of energy to the next level. By incorporating "Your Life Force," we gain deeper insight into the connection between our homes and our emotional well-being. Discover the power of Fung Shwa and learn how to use it to create a balanced and harmonized environment that supports your mind, body, and Soul.

The book explains the meaning of Sacred Fung Shwa to the Shamanistic principles that underpin it. Delve into the metaphysical medicine wheel and explore the elements of life, before moving on to practical applications of Fung Shwa in the home.

Learn how to visualize your home as a collective energy and clear the clutter to enhance its flow. Discover your Astrological colours and how they can be used in Fung Shwa design, from the kitchen to the bedroom and beyond. Explore the compatibility of personal colours in relationships, and discover the power of paintings, pictures, and mirrors to enhance your home's energy.

But Fung Shwa isn't just about the home—we also explore its applications in the office environment and in small retail businesses. Learn how to apply Fung Shwa principles to a clothing store, shoe store, or café, even discover the role of Fung Shwa in money, and to Metaphysical Numerology.

Throughout it all, we focus on the quest of life and how Fung Shwa can help you achieve your goals and live your best life. So what are you waiting for? Dive into the world of Fung Shwa and transform your home, your business, and your life today!

Book IX. Decoding Extra-Terrestrial Intelligence
Are you ready to embark on a journey of self-discovery? Look no further than O.M. Kelly's groundbreaking book, Book IX "Decoding Extra-Terrestrial Intelligence". Through metaphysical interpretation, O.M. Kelly (Omni) has unlocked the secrets of the universe and revealed that the key to our next step in human evolution lies within ourselves. This book will show you how to tap into the indelible imprint of holographic importance that is seeded within every human, and unleash the Extra-Terrestrial Intelligence that resides within you. Omni shares her own personal journey of encountering Beings of Light and how it has transformed her understanding of the universe and humanity's place within it.

Omni presents the concept that we all have Extra-Terrestrial Intelligence, and have the ability to tap into the vast knowledge and secrets of the universe. The ancient civilizations left behind clues and teachings about this metaphysical existence and it is up to us to continue to uncover and advance the way we think. Through this journey of life, we can unlock the secrets of our own consciousness and tap into the full potential of our existence. This is a fascinating exploration of the mysteries of the universe and the potential for our own personal evolution.

Readers who are interested in self-transformation through universal truths, Metaphysical exploration for personal growth and a journey of self-discovery would be interested in reading this insightful book on contact with Beings of Light and Extra-terrestrial Intelligence, exploring ancient civilizations and the knowledge they possessed about the universe and the human mind.

Power Thought for the Day Oracle Book

"Power Thought For The Day Oracle Book" provides insights to assist you on your life path. Through the "Totem" energy of all, the ancient species that have evolved before us, represent an emotional inheritance that we can rely on to sustain the moment. Each species that has evolved on this planet is recorded into our cellular memory. This book with 22 Major Arcana Shamanic Power Animal Totems provides a contemporary metaphysical interpretation symbolic of our evolution. By selecting a page of the book the Shamanic animal will provide an insight in how you are thinking at this moment in time. Through the contemporary Laws of Shamanism (with a metaphysical interpretation), O.M. Kelly (Omni) has produced a book that will assist the "Path of the Initiate" in emotional intelligence when our mind is in the field of doubt. When we become aware of how we are thinking it is a catalyst for transformation. This compact little book is a handy 4 x 7 inches or 10.2 x 17.8 cm to fit into your pocket or handbag.

How to use the book:
Our higher mind has no time; it steps into and works on behalf of the thought of the moment. This book encompasses 22 Major Totem Power representations, symbolic of our evolution. Close your eyes and inhale and exhale a deep breath and relax and allow yourself no thought as you select the right page of the Shamanic animal presented in this book. The right page will always appear for you at the right moment and you will discover how the power animals are working with you for insight into their wisdom. Different power animals come into our lives at various phases offering messages to guide us on our path.

Decoding the Shaman Within

In "Decoding the Shaman Within" international author O.M. Kelly (Omni) shares her Shamanic metaphysical journey. It would be termed a contemporary Shamanic initiation journey; a powerful spiritual enlightenment and transformational voyage of discovering the codes of Metaphysics and the Quest of Life. Through the sacred passage of time Omni discovered the secret codes of the Collective Consciousness (Laws of the Universe) to trek a higher level of consciousness. Throughout

Omni's training to receive the breath of Shamanism, many Elders from other cultures came to Australia and initiated her into their own tribal laws. Most of these Elders were men who arrived on Omni's doorstep uninvited but had received the call from the Universe to pass on their knowledge. Those magnificent people who had also earned their Shamanic experiences, only stayed long enough to give Omni their gift of consciousness and to initiate her into a new Shamanic name, which their tribe had bestowed, and then they disappeared out of Omni's life as quickly as they had come into it.

The Shamanic path in a Metaphysical perspective is the oldest pathway of the tribal law through the evolution of humanity. The Shaman is trained in the ancient language that is instilled in every genetic code that humanity carries within their DNA; you either have the opportunity to open it up and use it, or you just don't bother and choose to ignore it! It is as simple as that!

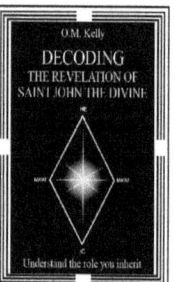

Decoding the Revelation of Saint John the Divine: Understand the role you inherit

The amazing breakthrough book "Decoding the Revelation of Saint John the Divine: Understand the role you inherit", is for anyone with an open, inquiring mind, seeking answers to the surreal descriptions of Earth's final days.

Through years of research O.M. Kelly interprets the cryptology behind the codes of mythology and various religions and has Metaphysically interpreted how the Holy Bible had been written through the original codex of Egyptology. The biblical stories were collected and condensed through the educated minds of that time.

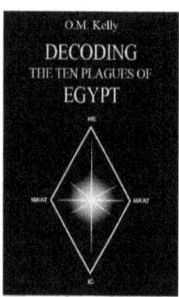

Decoding the Ten Plagues of Egypt

"Decoding the Ten Plagues of Egypt" presents a fresh insight into understanding the hidden structure of the language of how the Bible was written. The reader is introduced to the step by step Metaphysical decoding of the mystifying language, regarding the plagues from the Book of Exodus, Chapters: 7-12 in the Bible.

For the first time in contemporary history the essence of the Book of Exodus and its previously unsolved intriguing language will be revealed to provide deeper knowledge and clearer perception to unlock the significance the Book of Exodus is explaining to us.

Decoding Dreams

In "Decoding Dreams" international author O.M. Kelly (Omni), introduces a metaphysical interpretation of the dreams we dream. At times, we may believe that dreams allow us to peer into another world. O.M. Kelly provides the codes for us to understand that other world of dreams—or, through the Shamanic Principles, our "Vision Worlds". Dreams are created through your unconscious/higher mind communicating back to you; dreams are reminding you of the lessons that you need to understand regarding yourself. You cannot hear them if your mind is filled with incessant chatter. The ego refuses to conform when it is in control of the moment. Dreams can range from a pleasant dream, which could be a recommendation to add to what you are doing, to a nightmare, which is a wake-up call from your higher self regarding what you are doing to yourself. As you read this book, keep in mind that learning to metaphysically interpret your dreams is a step-by-step process. Areas covered in the book are: Dream Representations (Animal Kingdom and the Human Kingdom), Questions and Answers about Dreams, and Dream Interpretations.

Reprint coming in the near future.

www.ingramcontent.com/pod-product-compliance
Lightning Source LLC
Chambersburg PA
CBHW051538010526
44107CB00064B/2776